The Comeback Cat
Cleo's incredible journey through
feline diabetes to remission

By Heather Peden

Text copyright © 2016 Heather Peden.
All rights reserved.

Disclaimer

This is a story about my cat Cleo and our experience in successfully treating her diabetes.

I am not an animal health care professional, and as such the information in these pages is not intended as a substitute for veterinary care and should not be taken as professional advice in treating diabetes.

My hope in sharing Cleo's story is to entertain, to educate, and to give an example of what may be possible with the proper veterinary care. I also hope Cleo's story encourages pet owners to do their own research and to ask more questions of their veterinarians when it comes to the health of their animals.

The veterinary care and help we have received over the years for all of our animals has always been invaluable. I have an unending respect for the veterinary profession and the professionals who continue to help care for our pets. As with many diseases in both humans and non-humans alike, there are some conflicting ideas about how to treat feline diabetes. This book chronicles the road we decided to take with Cleo and its very positive outcome.

To all those who are better for having loved a cat.

Chapter 1

There is a gentle thump, thump, thump of tiny paws on the stairs leading to the bedroom. Each deliberate tread is gauged just so. Loud enough to disturb any last remnants of sleep but quiet enough to be passed off as an accident when paired with a feline face precisely arranged in an expression of startled confusion. "Oh, sorry, did I wake you?"

I lie in bed and listen to the soft pad, pad of carefully placed paws on the bare wood floor, squint open my eyes just enough to make out the shape of a cat slinking about the periphery of the room and then I close my eyes against the grey morning light at the windows, pretend I am still sleeping.

I can tell by the weight of the tread on the floor, the curve of the tail, the splotches of darker fur, like shadows mottling its surface, that it is Cleo. I smile into the covers pulled up to my face because Cleo has not done this for a very long time, come springing lightly into the bedroom. For months she couldn't even climb the stairs, leaving the top floor of our three-story house to her brother Chestnut. He happily stomped around the room in the mornings demanding breakfast before the sun was barely a wash of light in the sky, staring back with a shocked expression tending towards desperation when I fired at him, "Did the dogs put you up to this? What are they giving you?"

Cleo, for all her eccentricities – and there are many – has always been more polite about mornings and mealtimes. If she did appear beside the bed before the sun began to pale the sky I always believed it was more in the interest of doing a head count, making sure we were all still there, tiptoeing around the room and then out again. If she was hungry she would never say, just come running when she heard the rustle of the food bag or the plink-plink of kibble hitting her bowl as though her head was filled with too many other important things to worry about eating.

What she has excelled at over the years, and what was glaringly absent during the months when Cleo was in the very depths of diabetes, is her ability to drive everyone crazy for no particular reason at all. I thought of Cleo at one time as the kind of cat that could make you understand why some people don't like cats. If struck by just the right mood, she would sharpen her claws on various things, randomly pee on a towel forgotten on the bathroom floor, settle down on a pile of clothes in our room at bedtime to begin unnecessarily loud and rigorous grooming sessions, or wander the kitchen yowling, all forlorn and lost while everyone else sat upstairs in the living room.

"We're up here Cleo!" either my husband Morgan or I would yell and we would hear the scrabble of feet on the hardwood floor, the pick of claws on carpeted stairs as Cleo launched herself into the living room with an expression of relief on her face. "Oh thank goodness! I thought you had all been sucked into another dimension." But that is where her concern for our well-being ended and, secure in the fact that we had not just up and left her, she would stomp off with her rigid, no nonsense walk to peel more wood shavings from the banister.

These things though, these very Cleo things that have coloured her personality from the beginning, that have at times caused us to scratch our heads and at others driven us crazy, have felt very normal in their absence.

One night before she was sick, after Morgan and I settled in to bed to read, covers pulled up to our chests, the bedside lamp casting the room in a cozy orange glow, Cleo stomped up the stairs and marched stiff-legged towards a pile of clothes on the floor. I barely noticed her, my attention focused on the book I was reading, but something in Morgan snapped in that moment and in one motion he propped himself up on an elbow, extended his other arm like a whip and pointed a rigid, angry finger at her.

"Cleo, don't you even start," he said, the words tripping over each other in their haste. "Go." And he swept his pointing finger dramatically towards the door.

Without missing a step, Cleo pivoted abruptly and headed back to the stairs leading down to the living room with a couple of quick strides as though gearing up for a run, then slowed to a saunter that ended with her sinking to the floor as though she'd suddenly run out of energy. I looked up to see Cleo stretch out her then-voluminous body right at the top of the stairs, which is essentially a hole in the floor that reveals an alternate tread staircase, resembling a series of boxes stacked one atop the other, and plummets to the living room below at a very steep angle.

"Great. That's how we're going to die you know," said Morgan turning to me in all seriousness. "Tripping over a cat in the dark."

I immediately imagined the cats sitting around their water dish plotting our demise. But no, they are not malicious creatures, I thought as I looked at Cleo's grey and beige-splotched back, her head held at such a defiantly straight angle, her ears, one beige one grey, standing in a serious manner on her head.

Then again, at that time there was a lot about Cleo I felt I didn't know. Her brother was easy to figure out; he has always been fairly predictable with his constant need for validation, always present and engaged, but Cleo tended more towards mystery. I wondered sometimes if she did have a secret agenda. She always seemed to have one foot in another world somewhere, the only member of the family not present when humans, canines and Chestnut gathered in a social way. From the beginning, ever since she was a kitten, Cleo kind of went in her own direction, a bit of a stranger in our midst.

But then she got sick and became my main focus. I knew exactly where she was and what she was doing at every moment of the day. I got to know her quite well and to really appreciate her eccentricities, those quirky things that made Cleo remarkable, as they began to disappear beneath the weight of her diabetes.

So, when she appears in our bedroom this summer morning, light of foot as if it is nothing to flit easily from place to place, as if there were not a stretch of months behind her in which she sometimes couldn't walk across a room, let alone tackle the stairs, I don't care that it is early, that the trees outside our windows are still black silhouettes against a pale purple sky, I am just pleased that she is here.

There is a pause, the padding changes direction, comes closer, and then stops. When I open my eyes again, Cleo is sitting at attention on the floor beside the bed staring at me. Round, green eyes in a pale face alert and full of questions. Our mattress is positioned on a box spring that sits directly on the floor, a perfect height for impatient cats to peer in to sleeping faces.

When Cleo sees my eyes are open, she meows a short, sharp meow and leaps on to the bed, scrambles across my pillow and sticks her pink, wet, nose in Morgan's face. He pushes her away, mumbling, "Don't eat my eyeballs," in his customary fashion of believing the cats are just waiting for an unguarded moment on our part when they can begin feasting on us, and rolls over. Cleo turns to me again, clambers on to my chest and sits there looking down at me, purring a whisper of a purr.

In the lightening room Cleo's face is almost ghostly. A white triangle of fur peaks at her forehead, spreads across her nose, its other two points ending below her eyes. It is bracketed by swaths of light beige on her cheeks and muzzle, as though she has dipped her mouth and nose into a cup of milky tea. On top of her head the dusty grey that colours great sections of her fur sprinkles in with the beige and beneath her chin to her neck to her belly, pure white. I always think Cleo looks like a calico cat that has been left out in the sun too long, strong blacks and browns faded to a softer pallet. It is not until I start researching cats and diabetes that I learn she is actually called a dilute calico, which I love. It is as though she is a painting done in watercolours.

I watch her body rise and fall as I breathe and I think how different she is, how before we couldn't do this, when she was fat and balloon-shaped and her weight concentrated down into her tiny white feet making them four little pointy blades that she would awkwardly, almost spastically, dig into my flesh in some unrecognizable form of affection, as though she had read about it in a book somewhere. "This is how you interact with humans."

But she was too rough and mechanical and I would have to shove her off, almost involuntarily, in a flurry of self-preservation at which point she would stumble away down the bed, jump to the floor with a loud clonk and then go and sharpen her claws on the wall so one of us would have to bolt out of bed and chase her, "Or maybe this is how you interact with humans."

But since the diabetes, the weight loss, the regained mobility, the new lease on life, Cleo has become a completely different cat. She has become more social, more engaged in the life of our home, like she can finally admit she belongs here, that she is one of us. Perhaps she feels more like herself.

Cleo settles down on my chest, tucking her front feet beneath her as if she has crossed her arms in preparation for a long wait. Her eyes half-closed, her quiet purr vibrates softly through the blankets and I stay there for a while beneath her warmth and light weight, which must be a third of what it used to be, and I fall into a thin sleep, waking again when Cleo stands abruptly and tiptoes down the bed to the floor and then thump, thump, thumps her way back downstairs, her need for human interaction sufficiently topped up for now.

I don't know how a cat's memory works, what they remember of their day to day, if Cleo is aware that she was sick and now she is better. She acts like she knows, like she has been given back her body and look out because she is going to use it. She is going to run and leap and climb into laps and walk on counters and jump over dogs and catch mice and maybe climb trees. Maybe. And she is not going to let her brother beat up on her anymore. She will lay down the law before he even has a chance to think about it, swatting and hissing at him if he gets in her way, if he walks too close or greets her eagerly to find out where she has been.

"Get him Cleo," I used to cheer when she was the underdog and her brother, bigger and heavier, more solidly muscled, would jump onto her back, sink his teeth into her neck.

He would wait for her sometimes outside the bathroom door, crouched by the fridge, neck craned, head cocked, tail swishing. He listened for her approach and as Cleo marched purposefully in to the kitchen he would leap out of hiding, take a swipe at her as he landed and, caught by surprise, she would spring straight up in the air, all four paws leaving the floor at once.

Sometimes they would merge into a ball of flying fur and clatter and roll across the floor. There would be angry hissing and growling and yowling, mostly from Cleo, until I stepped in to break it up or the alarmed barking of a dog startled them out of the frenzy.

"Chestnut," I would snap as Cleo made a hasty retreat. "Don't be such a bully." And he would stare back at me, his amber eyes brimming over with innocence.

It is Cleo now I regularly admonish for being a bully as Chestnut approaches her with what I think looks like a friendly greeting, and she hisses and swats him in the nose before he even knows what hit him. But I suppose I can't really blame her. I have lost count of the number of times she has appeared over the years with a red-rimmed eye, half-shut and watering. "What did Chestnut do now?" I ask as she stares at me with her one eye, purring as though this is nothing out of the ordinary.

Deep down though I think they are still best friends. I have found them countless times sleeping together in a tangle on a pile of blankets or on the brown easy chair in the living room or on the bed. Faces pressed cheek to cheek, legs draped over necks, bodies enveloping each other. If they were the same colour it would be hard to tell where one cat ended and the other began, but Chestnut is all beige and stripy in varying degrees of depth. In some lights he is the creamy colour of rich caramel. I call him my little lion cub.

Chestnut and Cleo were littermates and have been together their whole lives. I suppose they might have somewhat of a love-hate relationship, their distinct personalities at once complementing each other and rubbing each other the wrong way. They are co-conspirators and adversaries, depending on the day and depending, I suspect in large part, on Cleo's attitude of the moment. Where Chestnut is fairly consistent and easy to anticipate, Cleo seems to change moods like they're outfits to be tried on, evaluated and discarded.

Cleo has always been fiercely independent, as a kitten shunning the company of her siblings to explore a quiet house alone at night, as an adult braving the slavering jaws of a wild puppy to ponder his impact on her existence while everyone else made themselves scarce, and as an ailing cat defiantly lurching through her days, hauling herself up the stairs one slow riser at a time, reveling in her ability to sleep away entire days.

She has never been shy about who she is, slipping in to new personas as she sees fit, as the mood strikes her or as life deals out a new hand. But this newest life she began, as her diabetes symptoms disappeared, is by far the most interesting.

Not only has she become more involved in our day-to-day lives, she also seems to have reverted to a younger, more playful self, bubbling over with energy. She often gallops about the kitchen on her own swatting a toy mouse or she searches me out so I will dangle a string in front of her nose or toss a coiled wire tag across the floor.

Perhaps she had a lot of time to think during her convalescence. Faced with the prospect of a life spent flopping like a fish across the floor from one box to another, struggling to stand at her food dish and never being able to climb the stairs again. I have to imagine she had some sense of what she used to be able to do and what was no longer possible. She seemed to accept her fate graciously enough though, as cats do, making the most of this suddenly abbreviated life.

But who knows what was going through her mind, because even though her physical abilities were deteriorating almost daily, that ailing life wasn't such a far cry from her other life as an obese house cat moving from one comfortable sleeping spot to another and another, following the sun as it moved across the sky and sent its warm yellow beams spilling over windowsills on to the floor or the back of the couch or the first riser on the stairs. For a number of years Cleo was a professional napper, surfacing from her dreams to yawn and stretch, eat a meal and occasionally demand a scratch behind the ears or swat and yowl at her brother for trying to start a fight before curling up again to chase sleep.

The cat that emerged from the other side of diabetes acts like she is making up for lost time.

Eleven months after Cleo's diagnosis and eight months since her body betrayed her completely, Cleo leaps one evening light-footed and almost silently into the bedroom. I have tossed the blankets on to the floor so I can remake the bed, lifting the sheet up in a big billowy sail and letting it fall in to place on the mattress.

"Hello Cleo," I say as she marches with purpose around to the opposite side of the bed surveying the situation, her face full of mischief, eyes round and black.

As I pick up the first blanket and billow it out over the sheet, Cleo springs up and slips easily beneath it and then spins and rolls and flings herself across the bed chasing the edge of the blanket as it unfurls around her with a snap. She catches it and bunches it up, wrapping her front legs around it and attacking it with rabbit kicks from her back legs. Her eyes wide and wild, she is like a kitten again, energy to burn, desperate to just play.

I want to scoop her up and hug her, but I am afraid to put my hands near, sure she will flip over and maul me instead. I throw another blanket over her and that one too is sucked into the center of the bed as though into a vortex before it has a chance to alight on the mattress and she has it bunched in with the first, a tangle of material that she kicks and bites in a frenzy.

"You're insane," I say to her as I wait for her to stop so I can pull the blankets off the bed again, start over. I put on a show of being exasperated with her, sighing loudly, pointing a finger at her, "Cleo, you are not being helpful," I say. But really I am elated. This cat, this energetic, mischievous, social animal feels like the cat Cleo is truly supposed to be and I am enjoying her immensely.

Chapter 2

At her worst, Cleo takes the form of a cat but the essence, that nimble, acrobatic fluidity that is the very definition of a feline, is gone.

She does not tiptoe unseen into a room, fading into the background until she decides it is time to be noticed. She clomps everywhere, the hocks of her back legs striking the ground with each step; her front legs bend backwards beneath her as though made of rubber. She walks like she wears flippers on each foot and as though she is trying to cut a path through two inches of molasses. We can hear her coming before she even knows she's on her way. I watch her face, the concentration set in her eyes, the effort she has to put in to just walking across a room.

In the mornings she emerges from her cardboard box in the kitchen. She humps out of it awkwardly as I descend the stairs from the living room above, and our bedroom a floor above that. She has always loved boxes, jumping into a new one before whatever was in it is taken out, and this box is the newest of many she has used over the six-and-a-

The Comeback Cat

half years we have lived in this house. Whenever the box is suitably used, lined with matted cat hair, sometimes stained with hastily cleaned up vomit, and starting to smell like wet cardboard, it is replaced by a new one. They have traditionally been shared by the cats, sometimes even at the same time, stuffed in there together in a swirl of overlapped furry bodies, a paw thrust into a face here, a leg thrown across a neck there. But since Cleo's illness the box has been hers alone.

I call it her safe place. It is where she beelines after breakfast with me hot on her tail with a syringe of insulin. Where it used to be a luxury, this box left on the floor for an afternoon nap, placed perfectly against the railing overlooking the entryway and the dogs and the comings and goings of everyone, wafted over with warm air from the woodstove by the front door, it has now become her bastion. I imagine she feels vulnerable just lying on the floor in an uncontained sunbeam, unsure of how quickly or reliably her body will respond in a pinch.

It is winter and still dark outside when I get up in the mornings, pick my way down the stairs into the lightless kitchen. Night still pushes in against the line of large windows, the forest right outside still hidden from view. But the dogs, two large black shadows, Murdoch and Molly, stir in the entryway at the sound of my feet contacting the wooden floor of the kitchen, Cleo rustles in her box and Chestnut thumps down the stairs behind me, having completed his task of getting me out of bed with his loud purr reverberating beneath the blankets.

The Comeback Cat

I flick on the light and the room becomes a glow of orange. Cleo clomps to the center of the kitchen, the halfway point to her dish in the bathroom, where the door can be closed and she can eat in peace without Chestnut nosing in to see if what she has in her dish is any better than what he has in his. It isn't.

Before I do anything else, I remove the small glass bottle of insulin from the fridge and roll it slowly between my hands. I have to do this each time to make sure the medicine is properly mixed together, since the insulin is a fine powder and does not actually dissolve in the delivery medium but remains suspended in it. I can't shake the vial as that would introduce air bubbles, and insulin degrades when it comes in contact with air. Also, shaking vigourously could actually break up the insulin molecules, rendering them useless.

I retrieve a miniature, cat-sized syringe from the small stash I keep on the kitchen counter and remove the orange protector from the sharp end and the squat opaque cover from the plunger end. I slide the needle into the grey membrane atop the insulin bottle, hold the bottle upside down and pull the plunger out until the tiny meniscus of the liquid reaches three units. I flick the syringe to dislodge any bubbles before removing the needle from the bottle and then I replace the orange protector and leave the syringe on the counter while I turn my attention to breakfast.

I open the cupboard under the counter with Chestnut weaving around my feet, cutting quickly in front of me and then back again, stretching up with his paws on the cupboard door as though trying to touch my cheek, turn my face to look him in the eye so he can convey his deep concern that his dish is empty and see if I truly understand the gravity of the situation. Cleo waits near the bathroom door following my movements with her eyes, sometimes sprawled out on her side if the effort of sitting becomes too much.

There are three big bags of crinkly food stashed in the cupboard. One for the dogs, who can eat just about anything, one for Chestnut who has a serious history of urinary crystals and is on a specific diet from the vet to help keep those from forming, and one for Cleo, a vet-approved kibble for diabetic cats.

I scoop a measure from each bag of cat food and dump it in their bowls. Chestnut eats below the windows against the wall. He dashes ahead of me as I carry the bowls, his tail standing straight up with a jaunty curve at the tip, his white paws, tap, tapping excitedly. I put his food down and turn to where Cleo waits by the bathroom, her green eyes brilliant and clear. She opens her mouth and a tiny squeak escapes. It is how she meows now, a half-thought as if bitten off in the middle, as though she has forgotten the words.

She stands, as much as her legs let her, and clomps into the bathroom, cozies up to her bowl when I place it on the floor, starts crunching on her breakfast right away.

In the beginning, I administered her insulin while she ate. The vet had suggested it; give Cleo a distraction. With her face lost in her bowl, I would kneel beside her and with one hand gather the skin at the back of her neck or between where her shoulder blades spiked up in little triangles while she ate and with the other hand slide the needle into her skin, press the plunger. It was over in a second, easy. But the very first time I gave her insulin, I was sure I did it wrong.

The needle is less than a quarter of an inch long and laser thin, its point disappears to almost nothing. That first time, when I gathered Cleo's skin between thumb and fingers and pushed the needle into her fur, I expected some resistance when it reached her skin and I expected a reaction from Cleo. But there was none, no pulling away or twitching or growling or hissing, and there was no resistance, no definite moment when the thin point of the needle contacted anything but air.

Cleo was eating her evening meal as I pulled at the skin on the back of her neck, she was even purring, which convinced me even more that I was doing it wrong. So I pulled the syringe back and tried again. Again there was no reaction, no resistance, but I assumed the needle was where it was supposed to be, so I pushed the plunger, removed the needle, checked her fur for dampness. It was dry, but the amount of insulin was so small, 2 units then, that I wondered if perhaps I wouldn't even notice it in her fur.

I stopped giving her insulin while she ate because it eventually began to annoy her. She would shift from side to side as I tried to pull at her skin and move her head in erratic patterns that made it difficult to hold on to her, so I let her eat in peace, closing the bathroom door until she was done.

When I let her out, syringe at the ready, she clomps to a stop a few feet from the bathroom door then sinks to the floor as though the effort of eating and then walking away from her dish has exhausted her. I kneel down beside her, run my hand over her head, she looks at me sharply and in a surprising burst of energy pushes herself to her feet and runs, in a flailing, stumbling kind of way, to her box, folds herself into it.

In her box she will let me do anything. I don't know if it is a resignation to her fate or if the security of the box gives her a sense of strength in the face of adversity, but once she is settled in she lets me pull at her skin and poke her with the needle without an ounce of fuss.

There are days, though, when she is feeling particularly uncooperative and will bypass her cardboard box and squeeze into the plastic cat carrier I have left sitting beside the water dish. I left it there because in the afternoons she seems to like to sleep in it, folded neatly on top of the red fleece blanket printed over with playful cats with balls of yarn and mice. Her head rests on the edge of the doorframe so she can see what is going on but is completely safe, contained inside her plastic box.

So it is, some days, that she seeks refuge inside the cat carrier as though she is making a statement of protest. "I can't run away from you and I can't really hide," she says. "But I can make this more difficult." Difficult maybe, but not impossible.

The Comeback Cat

"Oh, come on Cleo," I say when I see her veer last minute from her box and clomp the extra few steps to the carrier. She shuffles inside, turns around and settles down, her front legs folded beneath her, her face peering out at me with some indignation. I reach into the carrier holding the syringe backwards, pointed towards my body. I slip my other hand over her head and gather the skin, use my forefinger to probe the spot where the needle will go. I balance the hand holding the syringe with my pinky finger against Cleo's back to place it because I can't really see what I am doing, and then I pop the needle in where it's supposed to go and push the plunger.

"Thanks Cleo," I say, and then add, "Good kitty," as I always do and then pat her on the head and move away, let her slide into her morning nap.

Cleo sleeps a lot when she is in the midst of her diabetes. It is a different kind of prolonged sleeping than she used to do before she was sick. Previously, her lingering nap times were interrupted by bouts of engagement at key points of the day, a playful dash about in the kitchen after breakfast, a race to the top of the house, flying up the two flights of stairs, in which I imagined her creating a delusion of being a superhero with super fast reflexes, kind of like the Flash, a bid for the outside with kamikaze dashes at the open door, a coup launched among the dogs to stir things up a bit, get the adrenaline pumping.

And, on occasion, there were her valiant yet always doomed attempts to turn the tables on her brother. She would wait huddled outside the

The Comeback Cat

bathroom door for him to emerge, wiggling her body in anticipation as he entered the room in the very casual way he does everything. When she leaped out at him expecting, I imagine, to send him through the roof with fright, Chestnut would pause oh so briefly before swaggering past her with a glance of derision. I was always so disappointed for Cleo as she turned and scurried off to find a box to sleep in, perhaps give herself a pep talk.

But all these things stop when Cleo becomes diabetic, or at least when the diabetes progresses to the point that walking is an effort. It didn't start that way and I really have no idea when she crossed that line from being a healthy cat to being a diabetic cat. Although healthy here is a relative term. She obviously wasn't really healthy.

Feline diabetes mellitus can be a result of a number of things. It can be caused by diet and lack of exercise, but it can also be a secondary illness to the much more dire diagnoses of hyperthyroidism, pancreatitis, Cushing's disease. The vet tells us from the outset that Cleo's diabetes could be the very tip of a much bigger iceberg. We wouldn't know the cause for sure until we started treating it.

It happened both gradually and all of a sudden. One day she was climbing the stairs more loudly and slowly than normal and the next she was unable to jump on to the couch to sit beside me. I watched as she readied herself on the floor, stretched her neck, focused her eyes, and did that quick calculation in her head cats do when they judge a distance to be leaped. She aimed herself at the empty expanse on the seat next to where I sat with my legs curled beneath me, but when she launched, her back legs didn't have their regular oomph and the leading edge of the couch cushion caught her in the chest and bounced her backwards to the floor.

I laughed at first, the way you do at cats, those faultless creatures, when they trip over their feet or fall off the couch because they've rolled over too far.

"Did you see that?" I said looking up to where Morgan sat on his chair a few feet away thinking he would also find it funny. He didn't.

"That's not right," he said, looking troubled. And I stopped smiling, not knowing what to say as I watched Cleo shuffle off to find somewhere else to sit.

It was not the first time Morgan and I had seen Cleo's increasing disability differently. But he is generally more sensitive to these things. Born with Cerebral Palsy that affects his legs, Morgan walks with a limp, is a wheelchair-user and is intimately familiar with how disability can impact a life.

"She's walking funny," Morgan pointed out one day early on as Cleo clomped across the kitchen with her backend just inches off the floor, like a car whose suspension is going.

"No," I said. "She's fine." When clearly she wasn't.

But I have developed a strong sense of denial over the years. I maintain it was in response to Morgan's more alarmist personality. "I may over-react sometimes," he has said to me in the past. "But you are an under-reactor."

The Comeback Cat

I think it is probably something I have always done, deconstructing mountains down to molehill status. I have never been reactionary, and so I initially ignored the more severe slant to Cleo's back legs in what seems now like a perfectly foolish delusion.

"It's not that strange," I said as her legs thumped against the stairs like dead weight as she hauled herself up to the living room.

Because, on one hand hadn't she been slowing down anyway? Hadn't she been choosing the easier routes to get where she wanted to go for quite some time, climbing up on to the low living room windowsill and then onto the armrest of the couch to spread out across its soft pillowy back?

But when she sat on the steep stairs up to our bedroom, shuffling forward, then back, resting her front paw on the next riser up and staring longingly at the hole in the ceiling that led to the room with the big comfy bed and blankets for nesting, it was clear something was wrong. Even I couldn't deny that and when Morgan made the decision one day, picking up the phone while saying, "I'm calling the vet," I didn't argue.

"It's diabetes," the vet said the minute she saw Cleo clonking around on the linoleum floor of the exam room, before we barely had a chance to tell her our concern.

"We have to do blood work and urine analysis of course to confirm, but when the back legs do that, it's a clear sign."

The Comeback Cat

The three of us stood silently for a moment and watched Cleo clomp, clomp and shuffle her way from smell to smell in the tiny room.

It is called peripheral neuropathy, this weakness in Cleo's back legs, and in diabetic cats it is caused by prolonged hyperglycemia. The high levels of blood sugar in her system are damaging her nerves, interfering with their ability to transmit signals and interrupting their supply of oxygen and nutrients. Essentially, Cleo's legs aren't working properly because the very cells of her body are dying.

Diabetes. How did this happen? It is such a blow and we are suddenly caught up in a whirlwind of information as the vet explains what needs to be done next. First a blood test and then at home we will try and get a urine sample and the two things together will shape our next course of action

I feel a little stunned, but the vet is sweet and kind and naturally upbeat. She is the one who came to our house two years ago when we had to say goodbye to our beloved Bear, the very best dog that ever lived, and her gentle nature stretches forward to today leaving us with the thought that it is possible for diabetic cats, unlike humans or dogs, to go into remission.

Chapter 3

Remission. It sits like a tiny green island across an expanse of rolling grey ocean, a half-mythical place mentioned in passing, dropped discretely into conversation. It is a possibility, the vet tells us, if we can get Cleo's blood glucose levels under control. But she is quick to add remission is possible only if the disease is not caused by some as-yet-unknown underlying condition.

Time compacts around my heart, tightens. We are crunched down to this moment and the next moments strung out in a thin line before us. I want to start treatment immediately, what are we waiting for? The sooner we start the sooner she can get better. But it will take time to get the correct dosage of insulin, to track Cleo's sugar levels over the course of a day, a week, a month. But I want a solution now.

I cling to the idea of remission and at home I search the internet for any information that works in our favour. Remission is possible in some cases if the diabetes is caught and dealt with early enough, when there are still a number of undamaged insulin producing cells in the pancreas for the body to heal and start functioning more normally again. But what is early? How long has she been sick? I cannot find any definitive timelines.

Peripheral neuropathy is not the first indication of the disease. Early signs include excessive drinking, which I hadn't noticed, and dramatic weight loss, which I had.

My denial started immediately, if you can call it denial. I like to think of it as more of a best guess given the evidence at hand, although I turned out to be wrong. But when you have animals and have spent enough time around various minor concerns and patients who can't tell you exactly what, if anything, is wrong, you learn to not panic at the first pile of vomit or the lost appetite for one meal or the single spot of blood on the floor.

And Morgan agreed at first that there was no real cause for concern that Cleo had slimmed down rather suddenly.

"What happened to Cleo?" I said when I walked in the door mid-September, after a three-week absence visiting with a friend. The cat, who had always taken the shape of a well-inflated balloon, was suddenly half her "normal" size. When she sat down her back feet no longer disappeared beneath her overflowing white belly, her head did not look like a pin perched atop a bowling ball. I could see her waist.

This kind of drastic weight loss could not be a good sign. "I thought she was looking skinnier," said Morgan, who had spent the last three weeks with Cleo seeing her everyday and therefore had not really noticed her diminishing size, did not see it in the same shocking fashion I did having left behind a very fat cat to come home and find her very small.

But then Chestnut appeared beside her, huge and round and just about bursting out of his skin. If Cleo hadn't been right there I would have thought perhaps he'd eaten her.

I leapt to the most logical, and non-vet-involving, conclusion. Clearly Chestnut had been eating all the food again, pushing Cleo out of the way to stuff his face with not just his own meals, but hers too. I had seen him do it before which is one of the reasons the cats are separated during meal times, though we had become lax about enforcing that over the summer.

"Poor Cleo," I said. "She's starving!" But mystery solved, I thought, and decided to look on the bright side. Cleo needed to lose weight anyway and with her new size as a starting point I began separating the cats again. Cleo ate in the bathroom with the door closed, giving her ample time to eat at her own pace while Chestnut bolted his food in the kitchen then wandered around meowing for more.

When the cats were little, I reveled in their svelte shapes, their beautifully proportioned bodies, their movements like liquid. They skipped lightly across floors, tiptoed effortlessly along the edges of furniture, tumbled and sprang and leaped. They were these perfect little creatures of motion. I swore my cats would never get fat.

And then they did.

"Holy, do your cats ever miss a meal?" a visitor to our house once said when he saw the pair

The Comeback Cat

lumber through the kitchen when they were about four or five years old. I became embarrassed by their size.

I used to sit in the vets' office and look at the chart on the wall with the drawings of the top views of various cats showing the healthy sleek cat on the far left, progressing to the right with fatter and fatter cats until it got to the obese cat. I would try and convince myself my cats fit somewhere along the middle of the scale. I knew they were overweight, well overweight, and I had tried over the years to put them on diets, reducing the amount of food they ate each day, trying different formulas, meting out perfectly measured amounts to plink into their bowls at meal times. They were definitely fatter than they should be but were they really obese?

For a number of years, following their svelte days of effortless acrobatics, when they could be scooped up with one hand around their ribcages and slipped from my arms to the floor like pulled taffy, the cats settled into the roles of lazy housecats, which we facilitated at first by making sure they were well fed and satisfied.

I didn't like that they were becoming rounder and bigger but I appreciated their quietness, their reliability to sleep in puddles of sunshine, to emerge for food and then settle in for another nap because I was consumed by the big personalities of the canine members of the family.

There were three of them when we moved to our new house in the woods, Bear, Max and Murdoch. They were so different from one another. Bear, our Black Lab, was my soul mate and front and center of everything that went on in our lives, Max, our elderly German Shepherd adopted a year before the move, suffered from degenerative mylopathy that was stealing his ability to walk a little more each day, and Murdoch was the megalomaniac puppy-like creature I had found on the side of the road two months earlier who I maintain is part Giant Schnauzer, part dragon. He was essentially like a bomb going off in the midst of our lives.

In the whirlwind of dog, I was aware the cats spent their days following the little golden pools of sunshine that spilled over windowsills on to floors, on to the couch, on to the extra wide step that marks the corner of our stairs at the spot where they turn and descend from the living room to the kitchen.

Many a day we found a cat sprawled out in that most hazardous location, lethargic in the yellow warmth, a sleepy, drunken look on their face, the moment shattered in an instant with a grunt of discontentment as they were nudged forcefully from the spot by a foot looking to actually use the stairs for their intended purpose.

And I occasionally envied them those days as I wrestled yet again with the whirling dervish of teeth and claws that was Murdoch, cared for Max who soon needed a wheelchair to get around, made sure Bear did not feel overshadowed and forgotten. What must it be like to just collapse in a heap in any spot you want at any time because you're tired and the sun hits you just right and the house is quiet?

Compared to everyone else, the cats were relatively low maintenance. So, they napped and expanded and I eventually began to express concern for their weight, in particular on days when I would find Cleo sprawled out on the floor, her white belly a giant mound overtaking the rest of her colourful body, her profile somewhat reminiscent of a beached whale.

Attempts in the past to measure out their food and stick to regular feeding times had been short lived mostly due to our diminishing patience levels with all things pet, but after the baby gate incident I was determined to try again.

The gate sits at the top of the six steps that lead from the entryway into our kitchen. We put it there to stop Murdoch from taking over the entire house. He was so wild when I found him, with absolutely no regard for any other living creature, that initially he spent a lot of time in his kennel in the spacious entryway of our home. When he proved himself capable of being trusted to stay out of his kennel unattended, we still wanted to contain him in an area where we could control the amount of damage he inflicted on our things such as lifting his leg randomly around the house, eating small items of clothing, stealing loaves of bread off the counter, hence the baby gate.

It's one of those very basic wooden-framed ones with two plastic panels full of holes and two wooden arms that fold over each other, one with notches in it, the other with a metal hinge that drops into the appropriate notch so the panels can slide past each other and adjust to the width of the door frame.

After tripping over the gate and just about falling down the stairs in a tangle with the thing for the umpteenth time, Morgan finally fastened it to the wall with a hinge so we could use it like a door. He then cut a normal-cat-sized square hole in one bottom corner so Cleo, who liked to jump down between the spindles of the banister that overlooks the entryway from the kitchen and spend time with Murdoch, could escape when he got too rough, which he always did.

We often heard a plaintive meow, a gruff snarl, the scrabbling of feet on linoleum, the rattle of the gate as Cleo leapt through the hole and Murdoch planted himself on the stairs behind it. It seemed like an unnecessary risk to take, but Cleo insisted on repeating this scenario again and again.

It was on one quiet evening when I knelt before the pet food cupboard filling bowls for supper that Cleo had a falling out with the baby gate. Hearing the sound of food being dished, Cleo clambered up the stairs and I turned to watch her come.

Where I knelt put me directly in line with the hole in the gate and I waited as she began to climb through in her casual queen-of-the-universe kind of way. She reached through with her dainty front paws, followed by her head, then her shoulders, before coming to an abrupt halt. I watched as neck fat bunched at the back of her head and she reached forward with her front paws and tried to pull herself through while at the same time shoving with her back feet on the first step down.

She rocked back slightly and then gave a couple of good, full-body shoves forward before the momentum of her efforts caused the gate to begin to swing slowly open. Her eyes widened as her front paws scrambled to hold on to the kitchen floor and pull herself forward again, but she pushed herself farther away instead. When her back feet slipped off the top step, her front legs were extended as far as they could go, her toes strained to hold on, her face fixed in concentration.

In retrospect, I could have helped her then, held the gate steady for her to maneuver through instead of watching with some fascination as her paws finally lost contact with the kitchen floor and the gate continued its slow swing away from solid ground. Cleo hung for a moment about a foot above the second step down as the gate came to a stop. She was folded completely in half, her front end on one side of the gate, her back on the other. It looked like she was straining to touch her toes before she managed to slither through, front first, and drop down to the stairs with a gentle thud. As casually as though she was a seasoned celebrity who'd just pulled up to the curb in a limo and was greeting a mob of over-exuberant fans, Cleo hopped up the last couple of steps to the kitchen and sauntered towards her food dish with an air of having everything completely under control.

It was hilarious and sad all at the same time. Morgan suggested widening the hole when I told him later what happened. I was completely opposed to the idea. How ridiculous, I thought. I am not making a perfect, cat-sized hole bigger because my cat has become too large to fit through it. She just has to return to her former cat-sized self.

That was easier said than done and when we eventually did have to enlarge the hole for Cleo so her escape route was still an escape route, since she was determined to spend a lot of her time with the unruly Murdoch, I decreed something was going to change. I bought a diet kibble, returned to measured quantities, and the cats became outraged. The measured amounts grew a little bit more each time, an extra meal or two were occasionally thrown in when the cats were particularly insistent and annoying, marching around the kitchen with harsh cries of protest, raiding the cupboards, ripping chunks out of cardboard boxes, chewing on the edge of the table or books or even feet. We sprayed them with water, yelled into incredulous faces, tried to ignore them until it became a hazard with cats throwing themselves at our feet so we would trip and send the cat sliding across the room, claws scrabbling at the wood floor for purchase.

The diet thing didn't work so well. And when we did manage to find a balance of meal times and amounts, they still didn't lose any weight.

The battle continued for five years. The cats just turned nine when Cleo suddenly slimmed down and Chestnut ballooned. And even though I thought I had explained it away, I still kept a close eye on Cleo, seeking her out in the house and paying her more attention. I wasn't completely unworried.

She didn't bulk up again, but I noticed a patch of hair missing from one of her front legs. That, I chalked up to stress from being half starved because the fur seemed to be growing back in again now that she was actually getting something to eat. And then the leg thing started.

It is December when we finally take her to the vet. Three months after the weight loss and who knows how many months since she actually developed diabetes. The vet asks about excessive drinking and if we noticed the litter box needing changed more frequently.

"No," I say, wracking my brains. Were there other signs? "I fill the cat's water dish a lot," I say. "But that's because the dogs always drink it." And they do, draining it every time as though it is not the same water that fills their own dishes in the entryway, as if it somehow tastes better.

The cat litter, I explain, is sawdust and wood shavings from Morgan's sawmill, both of which become saturated quickly and therefore I am frequently changing the litter, but I can't say it is because it is being used more often.

No, the biggest indication that she was unwell was the way her legs suddenly began to clonk awkwardly when she walked and I stalled because I really didn't want something to be wrong with this cat who has been hardly any trouble her entire life with us, the only one to never need the vet.

Except for occasionally letting her frustrations be known by peeing on random things, Cleo could mostly be counted on to be low-maintenance, frequently taking on the role of disinterested housecat, pretty much the exact opposite of Chestnut.

Chestnut, who is more social, clingier than Cleo, has also been more susceptible to stressful situations over the years resulting in a chronic urinary crystal problem which reared its ugly head pretty much every two years like clockwork.

The worst bout was his first one when he was two and a half years old and I brought Murdoch

The Comeback Cat

home seat-belted into the car after plucking the overgrown puppy from the side of the road where I imagine he had been left because he was insane. We were renting a tiny little box of a house at the time and Murdoch was like a live firecracker the moment he charged across the threshold straight into Bear and Max, who tried to scatter in the cramped space, ears pinned back, alarmed expressions plastered to their faces.

Chestnut, we discovered later, made a hasty retreat beneath the couch and stayed there, even after we brought in the big metal kennel to contain the beast. With this new high-intensity interloper in our midst, we didn't even notice Chestnut was having a problem until we found blood outside the litter box a few days later, realizing too late that Chestnut had not been drinking any water or using the box regularly.

He was hospitalized with a urinary catheter to empty his bladder, put on medication and switched to a special food that was supposed to break up and prevent the formation of crystals. It sort of worked, but Chestnut continued to live on the brink of another attack with any one stressful event threatening to tip him over the edge, like moving house, or a particularly violent wind storm, or introducing another new dog to the family.

Meanwhile Cleo remained unflappable and set up shop in front of Murdoch's kennel, sprawled out just inches away from the door watching him with a relaxed curiosity as he barked and lunged, rattling and clanging the big metal cage.

The Comeback Cat

I don't know if it happened then or later, but somewhere along the line Cleo's fascination for this new dog grew in to something like affection and she became determined to spend time with him even as he threatened to eat her. It was almost like a life mission.

When we moved to our new house, a tall, window-laden structure nestled in the woods, our couch, which had taken quite a beating from all the dogs and cats that had traipsed across it over the years, was relegated to the entryway with Murdoch until we could decide what to do with it. Cleo spent a lot of time underneath it. I imagined she fancied herself a scientist, obscured by her cleverly camouflaged blind where she could sit and make her observations of this curious dog.

One day, a few months after moving in, I sat on the floor with my back against the couch, Murdoch sprawled at my side with his body stretched the length of my legs. He had just recently become manageable enough that I could sit with him for short periods of time without being mauled.

I tried to embody calm and spoke quietly to him while he writhed around on the floor as though trying to keep the demons from taking possession of his body again. I rubbed his chest and his ears, letting his manic energy bounce off of me and began to enjoy a few quiet moments with this problem dog. It didn't last long.

I heard a loud scrabble under the couch. A split second later, I looked down and there was Cleo on her back, claws sunk into the front of the couch where she had grabbed it and slid along the floor

The Comeback Cat

propelling herself out from under her safe haven well past her shoulders. Everybody froze. Cleo stared at me as though she had no idea how she got there, and then glanced at Murdoch whose head whipped around on his shoulders to look at her, though he still laid on his back. Not even the air particles moved around us for that moment when no one dared to breathe.

I had just a flicker of a thought to get out of the way before the scene exploded. I made a hasty retreat as Murdoch dove under the couch where Cleo had just disappeared again. He was too big to fit right under it, so Cleo sat against the wall at the back of the couch and taunted him. It entertained her for hours.

Cleo has emerged from the entryway over the years in various states of disarray, with slobber plastering her hair this way or that, her side glistening where Murdoch's drool landed after flying from a barking mouth. She has arrived calmly in the kitchen following explosions of clattering metal and feet skittering across linoleum when Murdoch charged from his kennel as Cleo paraded by, taunting him.

So, when Cleo began having trouble getting around, when her back legs didn't seem to work quite right anymore, I found it hard to believe that anything could really be wrong with this brazen cat who wore dog slobber like it was some sort of badge of honour and who regularly took on an animal seven times her size, with giant teeth and an unreasonable streak a mile wide.

But there's the weight loss and her legs and the blood work from the vet shows a blood glucose level of 27 millimoles per litre (mmol/L) when the normal range, I discover much later, is anywhere between 2.6 and 8.4. We just need a urine sample to 100 per cent confirm that it is diabetes and to check for ketoacidosis, a potentially life-threatening complication of uncontrolled diabetes where ketones build up in the blood and urine as a by-product of fat being broken down for fuel since the body is no longer able to use glucose. In high concentrations, ketones are poisonous.

Chapter 4

I wake up early to stalk the litter box. The cats blink sleepily at me when I turn on the kitchen light and then wrap themselves around my legs even though their official breakfast time is still a couple of hours away. I put down food for Chestnut in the kitchen and take Cleo into the bathroom. It is the coldest room in the house, tacked on to the kitchen and full of windows. It is a beautiful room. The forest marches right up to the house and if it is daylight, you can have a bath while looking up into the trees.

I sit on the closed lid of the toilet seat, look at my huddled reflection in the black of the night-darkened windows, and watch Cleo eat. When she is done, she will use the litter box. That's her routine, though the day before she did things backwards which is why I am up before the sky begins to lighten, sitting in the cold bathroom half asleep, waiting for my cat to pee.

The sterilized collection cup with the orange lid sits on the countertop beside me; I have taken the top off the covered litter box in the corner. If this goes smoothly, I may be able to sneak back to bed for a few hours.

Cleo finishes eating, eyes the wooden laundry box with Morgan's clothes from the day before piled on top, and then turns and sits by the door.

"You should pee Cleo," I say and she looks at me with her round green eyes. We stare at each other for a moment and I know it is futile so I open the door and we leave the bathroom together.

I dish myself some yoghurt with blackberries, put the kettle on for tea because it is cold, and eat quietly at the table. Chestnut sits on the chair next to mine, his chin just an inch above the tabletop, and watches me eat by the lonely yellow light of the kitchen. When I'm done, he gets the bowl and I wander over to the railing that overlooks the entryway.

I stand looking down into the darkness with the kitchen light at my back. I am wrapped in a blanket, the hood of my sweatshirt pulled up over my head, as I lean against the wall.

I can just make out Cleo's lighter coloured shape stretched out beside Murdoch's dark one. I know it is Murdoch even though it is Molly's bed because he is curled into a ball the way he does when the house is cold, which it was when I stumbled down the stairs at 5:30 in the morning, the fire burned out so that only the tiniest coals winked weakly when I opened the door of the woodstove, reached in with the metal prod and stirred them up, raked them forward and opened the damper wide, selected the smallest bits of wood from the cart, peeled some birch bark and tossed it in.

The Comeback Cat

There is a faint orange glow visible through the glass of the stove door indicating heat to come, but my eyes are trained on Cleo, trying to decide if she is settling down for the long haul. She spent the entire day before on that bed while I hovered about waiting for her to do something: lid off the litter box in the bathroom, collection cup standing by.

Behind me the kettle is starting to boil and I make myself a cup of tea instead of a pot, still convinced I may be returning to bed before the day really starts.

I sit at the table and I read, my feet up on the chair where Chestnut sits waiting for something interesting to happen. I sip my tea as the minutes tick by and the blackness at the windows fades to indigo and still Cleo does not pee. "This is insane," I say to the room.

And then Molly's dark face with the tall German Shepherd ears appear at the baby gate at the top of the kitchen stairs and there is no denying the lightening sky and the snowy white woods outside the window emerging from the black. I can hear Morgan upstairs getting out of bed and the day officially starts.

The dogs go out, come in, get breakfast and the cats get second breakfast. I carry Cleo into the bathroom and set her down in front of her dish and then I am sitting in the bathroom for the second time this morning waiting for my cat to pee. And then she does, wandering casually over to the litter box, spinning around once, then squatting. I kneel down with the cup, slide it underneath her and catch the sample I've been waiting for. Until now I hadn't known if she would let me do this. I have never needed a urine sample from Cleo before.

For Chestnut and me this is old hat. He is used to me holding a cup beneath him. I have collected numerous samples from him over the years as he battles through another round of urinary crystals. I am lucky he is so amenable. But Chestnut is a special case; I often call him my posable cat. I can do just about anything with Chestnut and he lets me. I can sling him over my shoulder and he hangs there like a scarf, I can roll him on to his back and poke him in the belly and he just looks at my finger with mild curiosity; I can stand him on his back legs and from behind use his front paws to make a speech or sing a song or make him dance. If he's melted across my lap on the couch, I can lift him and place him beside me, go do something, come back, and replace him on my lap and he just stretches and groans and usually purrs incredibly loud.

Cleo is traditionally not so easy going about things, more inclined to bolt from my lap if I so much as change the rate of my breathing than to wait and see if I was just going to tell her that she is beautiful. She's not really difficult, she just seems to have a higher standard of self-preservation, perhaps a healthier dose of suspicion, and I wasn't sure she would let me intrude on her litter box time. But she does, surprisingly, and I screw the orange cap back on the cup and hand it to Morgan as he heads out the door to drop it off at the vet clinic on his way to work.

The sample is the last piece of the puzzle that confirms without a doubt that Cleo has diabetes. She does not have ketoacidosis, but the sample does confirm a bladder infection, which is a common side effect of diabetes due to the high sugar content in the urine creating a perfect medium for the growth of bacteria.

For the last two days I have been researching feline diabetes. The information I find online about treating it is scattered and full of opinions and I am quickly overwhelmed since we don't yet have all the information about what is actually happening in Cleo's body. But I skim through various explanations about the mechanics of the disease and read that, just like humans, cats can either have insulin-dependent type I, or non-insulin-dependent type II.

I read about how insulin, the hormone that shuttles glucose into cells for fuel, is no longer being produced by the pancreas or is being blocked from entering the cells somehow so glucose builds up in the blood. The cells, deprived of this 'food', essentially begin to starve and the liver, kidneys, and circulatory system become overtaxed trying to deal with all the extra glucose floating around. The cells, in search of fuel, will turn first to stored fat and then to muscle to get the energy they need to continue living. I read that diabetes in cats is on the rise and that, unlike dogs and humans, cats can indeed recover from it. Their bodies can be encouraged to start working normally again.

I discover through a couple of online sources that a wet-food exclusive diet is highly recommended, not only for diabetic cats but also for healthy cats. Felines, these websites admonish, should never eat kibble. They are obligate carnivores, designed to get all the sustenance they need from eating meat. Their bodies are particularly well suited to breaking down meat proteins into the necessary elements needed to survive, including glucose.

I flip from page to page on the internet, opening more links, filling my brain, until I can't separate the useful from the frivolous, until I finally step away from the computer because I think I am re-reading information I have already read and I can't really do anything more until we start treating Cleo and see what happens.

Now that we have confirmed Cleo's diabetes with the urine sample, we are scheduled to return to the vet that day for an instructional visit on how to administer the insulin Morgan picked up from a pharmacy in town.

We load Cleo back into the carrier and drive the short distance over country roads, packed white with snow and shiny in spots, to the vet clinic with mournful meows coming from the back seat. The road takes us down the mountain amidst the burgeoning evergreen and white-trunked trees of the boreal forest, rock giving way to flatter land, forest petering out to open farm country tucked in for the winter beneath a thick blanket of snow.

The vet clinic is a tiny house on the edge of a farm. It is immediately surrounded by flat fields with a mountain directly behind it, part of the Nor'wester range that curves around the land in a great sweeping arc and runs away towards Lake Superior in the distance and the southern edge of Thunder Bay.

It is a beautiful spot and I love coming here, except of course for the purpose of our visits. I don't love that part. But it is a pleasure to stand outside with my dogs, wander the grassy spots beneath spreading pine trees or – if I'm with Murdoch and I have to take him away from the building to await his turn because he does not always mix well with other dogs – walk between the straight rows of apple trees in the tiny orchard just across the creek that runs alongside the clinic.

It is right at the end of the day when we arrive with Cleo. We are ushered straight in to an exam room where the vet and a vet tech go over how to administer the insulin using a saline solution in a syringe. We are handed a neon green piece of paper covered over with uniform, square letters in blue ink. It is almost too perfect to read. The information there outlines what we know so far about Cleo, what her sugar levels are (27.4 mmol/L), what we should aim for (5.5-16.7 mmol/L), and dosages and times for insulin.

We start with 2 units. A miniscule amount, the vet shows us, in the tiny syringes Morgan also picked up at the pharmacy. We are instructed on how to store the insulin, how to prepare it every day, and the best place to give it to the cat, which we are told is the scruff at the back of the neck.

We are also prescribed a special diabetic cat food. It is in kibble form. I hesitate for a minute, debate whether or not I should say something, whether or not to question this food choice. But as we are gathering up our things and Cleo has been wrestled back into her carrier I have to ask.

"I was researching diabetes online," I say, somewhat sheepishly, almost apologetically, because everybody is suddenly an expert with the internet and forget about the fact that you went to veterinary school. "There were some suggestions about switching the cat to a wet food only diet. Do you think we should try that?"

The vet cocks her head to one side, lips pursed as though considering the question and then almost imperceptibly shakes her head. "No, I don't think that's a good idea," she says, and then explains that a diet without the hard kibble to help clean teeth could lead to bad oral health, which can be a precursor to a host of other problems.

"Oh, okay," I say, though I am not completely satisfied with this answer and only partially because Cleo's teeth are already not in great shape after eating kibble for her entire life.

But everything is so new. I just learned how to give insulin to my cat and there was talk about eventually learning how to do home glucose testing, and there is still the possibility that the diabetes is just a symptom of some other problem yet to be determined. So, we buy the bag of cat food, pay for the medication to treat the bladder infection, gather up all our stuff, and bustle Cleo back out to the car.

We return home with all our instructions, the insulin and syringes. A giant yellow sharps container is installed beneath the vanity in the bathroom. It is about the same size as the cat and I imagine taking it to the beach to make sandcastles. It was all they had at the pharmacy even though each syringe we will be using is only slightly bigger than a golf pencil.

During the first two weeks of Cleo's new life, she is suddenly cast as the leading player in our home. It is strange for me how quickly everyone else fades to the background and my world begins to revolve around Cleo, when it used to be the opposite. I plan my days around feeding times and insulin shots and the medication for her bladder infection. I watch her closely as she moves from box to food dish to the stairs, at the bottom of which she often sits contemplating the climb before starting the long, clattering journey to the top.

In the living room, I help her on to the couch or make sure the way is clear for her to find her path from the floor to the low windowsill to the arm of the couch and then on to the cushions of the back where she can stretch in a patch of sunshine and look out the window or curl up beneath the lamp. And I sit beside her frequently giving her ear a scratch, frequently asking how she is. She looks back at me with a pleasant expression, green eyes like painted porcelain relaxed, and I take that as a "thanks for asking."

Before this, sometimes days would go by when I barely saw Cleo at all. She would regularly appear in the kitchen at the plinking sounds of kibble being measured into her dish after Chestnut had spent the previous hour stomping in circles around the house, throwing himself dramatically in front of any human or dog who might, just maybe, notice that he was starving to death yet again and finally do something about it. But Cleo would spend her day tucked away in some corner of our small home, inside a drawer left open in the bedroom, on a pile of blankets on a chair, under the couch in the entryway, in the crawlspace beneath the kitchen, doing whatever it was Cleo did with her hours.

The Comeback Cat

There were other times when she would always be there, just in the background, busily marching from room to room, looking like she had some heavy things on her mind and was engaged in something terribly important. She would ignore everybody around her as though she had far too many pressing things to do and absolutely no time for social niceties.

But then she would occasionally storm into a room and demand short, intense bursts of attention, throwing her bulk against legs, circling on tiptoe, meowing a clipped, intense meow before abruptly marching off with great purpose to climb into the cardboard box of crinkly old wrapping paper and stare wide-eyed at the ceiling. These kinds of displays would prompt Morgan and I to renew our discussion of her oddities. We have wondered about her over the years, wondered about things like what planet she might be from and if she was perhaps waiting for the mothership to return.

She went through a phase when she barged her way on to my lap every morning just about knocking the mug of tea out of my hand and meowing her "I have something earth-shattering to tell you," meow, clinging to me like a person drowning, nose rammed into my face, claws grasping at my shirt. And then one day she suddenly stopped with no warning or outside influence.

Shortly after that I watched her one morning from the kitchen table as she stomped past me with great purpose on a beeline from the baby gate to the bathroom, her shoulder blades rhythmically counting off each stride. A few minutes later she returned on the same path, stomp, stomp, stomp. She seemed to be pacing off times and distances.

"Cleo, what are you doing?" I asked, as she thumped past again. She ignored me completely as though her head was full of calculations and she couldn't possibly stop now, especially not for frivolous things like back scratches or loving head-butts.

At times over the years, I have found Cleo hard to relate to. She either made herself invisible, slinking about the house as though a secret agent on a life or death mission, or else everything was urgent and alarming and she existed in a prolonged state of desperation. Her attempts to interact with the other members of the household were just awkward and clingy. Mostly she molested people and the dogs, weaving her then-voluminous body manically around legs becoming a very serious tripping hazard.

I just didn't get her. I wanted to understand her over the years, but there was a barrier there, some social awkwardness that prevented me from really getting to know her. It became easy to dismiss her as a strange little cat as she went about her own business, never really needing anything from us, except the occasional validation of acknowledgement, as the rest of the animals vied for attention, needed special care, or demanded extra patience.

So, as this new phase of Cleo's life began with me watching her every move, keeping track of what she ate and where she slept and what she could and couldn't climb, and her responding with a quiet affection, I felt like I was finally seeing her true personality and I wondered if perhaps I had taken her a bit for granted during the first nine years of her life, dismissing her as anti-social, assuming she didn't need us at all when really she just didn't need us in the same way as everyone else.

Chapter 5

If Cleo had any qualms at all about my renewed interest in her, she never said. Her relaxed approach to suddenly being the center of attention may have been a result of not feeling like herself, the diabetes taking away a lot of her energy, but I like to think she was pleasantly surprised by her new role of star housecat considering she had always been socially awkward and a bit of an outcast from the very beginning. Basically, she became part of our family because nobody else wanted her.

Cleo came to us the way almost all our animals have, by happenstance. She appeared in my life one September morning with five other peeping, squeaking kittens inside a cardboard box in the magazine section of the bookstore where I worked.

The store had just opened for the day and I was off in some far reaches of the building shelving books when one of the managers approached.

"Morgan's here," he said, pausing, then added with a question, "and he has a box of kittens?"

The Comeback Cat

"What?" I said, dropping what I was doing and hurrying to the front of the store.

The box of kittens sat on the pale wooden floor surrounded by women, my co-workers, laughing and cooing and fawning all over them. I looked down at the tiny furry bodies reaching up the sides of the cardboard, peeping like chicks and I smiled somewhat woodenly as hands reach down to scoop them up, bring them to rest against necks.

I had expected to see Morgan that morning, to hear about his visit to the Humane Society. We had been fostering a dog for the previous seven months, a mature Border Collie/Lab-cross named Quincy who had recently developed an abscess in his neck. The vet told us he needed surgery, but that was not our decision to make since he did not officially belong to us, so Morgan took him in to the Humane Society that morning for them to have a look and decide what to do. Kittens had not been anywhere on our radar.

I looked at Morgan, eyebrows raised, with an expression of incredulousness on my face. Morgan stood back and beamed at me a knowing smile, and explained how a woman brought in this box of kittens while he sat waiting with Quincy. "But they wouldn't take them," he said. "They told her to take them to Animal Services, but she didn't want to do that. I sat there and listened to them argue back and forth and then I finally said I would take them."

He seemed quite pleased with himself, but I was speechless, wondering what on Earth he had been thinking as I looked from Morgan to the box with the thought, 'I do not want these kittens!' blaring like an alarm through my mind.

The Comeback Cat

We had come to Thunder Bay nine months earlier, renting a tiny house outside the city on the edge of the Current River. It was Morgan, Bear, and I and we had planned to stay for just a few months before moving on, headed west in the direction of the Territories and Alaska, after setting out from the east coast a year before. We had already spent months camping and paddling canoes and living out of my car as we explored one back road after another.

Thunder Bay, the mid-point of the country, seemed like a good place to stop for a while. And it was on Lake Superior, whose big water we had fallen in love with after a paddling excursion in the fall that took us a ways along the north shore. It was wild country and we wanted to see more of it.

As waterways froze and snow piled up in towering drifts at the side of the road, we found the little house to rent and I got a part time job while Morgan went back to college for a semester, but I always had one foot out the door with my bag packed and Bear's squeaky fish at the ready because once summer came, in my mind, we were going to be back on the road.

As that nomadic life beckoned to me, however, just two months in to our stay Morgan was feeling large of heart and wanted to foster a dog from the Humane Society. Bear and I were dubious about it with me saying, "But we're not staying," and Bear saying, "But you have me!" and, really, what else did we need?

Our little house on the river near an old hilly clear-cut patterned over with trails was a perfect spot for a dog who needed a home, even for just a little

The Comeback Cat

while, argued Morgan. So, we contacted the Humane Society, did a little research, and found Quincy.

He was the only dog at the Humane Society not climbing the walls of his kennel. Instead, he lay motionless, chin resting on paws, staring into the distance. We took him home that afternoon and he spent the evening under our bed, where his bones rattled against the bare wood floor. Bear lay on the couch in the living room, shooting sideways glances at the bedroom as if to ask, How long is he staying? They rode home together in the back of the car, Quincy ignoring us all and Bear trying to make herself as small as possible in one corner of the back seat so she didn't have to touch him.

It took a few months but Quincy who was shy and skittish at first and who preferred to spend the bulk of his days outdoors visiting the neighbours or quietly contemplating life on the lawn, slowly relaxed in to life with us that summer. And when we were still living in that little house on the river by August it was clear we weren't going anywhere right away so we started talking about adopting Quincy.

It was right around then Quincy showed up one morning with a swollen head. I thought at first he may have had an allergic reaction to a bee sting, but then it turned out to be an abscess in his neck which led us to the vet and then took Morgan to the Humane Society and brought the box of kittens in to our lives.

Morgan's plan with the kittens, he later explained, was to bring them to the bookstore where everyone was gaga for animals. He imagined them all falling in love with the kittens, everyone agreeing to take one and within moments he would have found them all homes, leaving our two-dog family intact.

Even though his reasoning seemed fairly sound, I was annoyed in that moment that he had agreed to take these tiny, needy creatures that were too young to not have a mother, theirs having disappeared one day leaving the kittens alone in a tree house in someone's backyard. What about our plans to not get too attached to anything here? Our plans to get back on the road? The box felt like an anchor around my neck.

I stared into the face of a little beige kitten with dark blue eyes and ears that had not quite unfurled to their proper position on top of its head. I kneeled down and cupped my hand beneath him, lifted him from the box and watched as the women cooed and laughed and fawned over the kittens that now, somehow, belonged to me.

What are we going to do with a box of kittens? What was Morgan thinking? And I felt the tiny vibrations of the beige kitten against my neck and I knew then if we kept any of these kittens, it would be this one.

The kittens were returned to the box. There were six of them. Two orange, two dilute calicos, one regular calico and the beige one. We closed the flaps of the box against the peeping clamour from inside and Morgan left for home with promises from all the women to take a kitten in a few weeks when they would be old enough to be re-homed.

So we added six kittens to our family and at home we set the kittens up in a bigger box with a towel at one end and newspaper at the other and a tin plate filled with shredded newspaper inside as a hopeful makeshift litter box. But they did not know how to use a litter box yet and each morning we found the towel beneath the heap of kittens soiled and needing washed.

They huddled together in their box and scrabbled at its sides when we pulled open the flaps each morning, letting in the light. Just like little birds, the minute we covered their lair with a towel for the afternoon or evening they stopped their peeping and mewing, which was otherwise constant.

We fed them milk replacement by syringe, each of us plucking a peeping kitten from the box, cupping them in one hand by their little bellies and with the other carefully depressing the plunger to mete out the liquid into eager mouths. Morgan sat on his chair while I perched on the edge of the couch scooping up kittens one at a time as though they were on an assembly line. We held their wriggling bodies while the room filled with hungry, high-pitched mews that left us wondering if we'd fed them enough.

Quincy, in the midst of all this, made himself scarce most of the time, preferring to sit outside or hang out in the bedroom while Bear satisfied her curiosity when the kittens were still tiny balls of fur that peeped inside their cardboard box. She gave them a good sniffing and then dismissed them as uninteresting and nothing to do with her. So she staked out her spot on the couch, high above the troupe of furry circus performers who were still too small to climb.

The Comeback Cat

But as they grew, they quickly became little explorers, marching along the floor with purpose as though setting off across a vast desert, or tromping over blankets like mini-mountaineers, or scaling the couch with their tiny little nails as though it were a cliff-face.

There were three boys and three girls and they all instantly had their own personalities but I did not want to name the kittens, not really. I didn't want to get overly attached to them. But we started referring to the two orange males as Dr. Evil and Mini Me, after the characters in the Austin Powers movies. Dr. Evil, almost twice the size of everyone else, was clearly the bully, throwing his weight around and stepping on his siblings without batting an eye. Mini Me was the runt of the litter but looked just like his much bigger brother.

The kitten who would become Cleo was a curiosity. From the beginning she was different. She was the second smallest of the bunch and seemed to be the brunt of her siblings' jokes. It was she we would find wandering around the living room after all the kittens had been tucked inside their fortress-like box for the night and we imagined the others had hoisted her up and out through the cardboard flaps, a practical joke that started with them getting her excited about a covert mission.

Twice we found her with not a wisp of a whisker left on her face. I have no idea what happened, but again we pictured the others ganging up on her, holding her down and chewing them off. She seemed completely unconcerned by the whole thing, staring at us blankly as we questioned her about where her whiskers were.

And then, not long after, she had a fall that I maintain jolted her brain just enough to colour her personality and shape her into the eccentric cat she would become.

The kittens had quickly grown into acrobatic explorers, infiltrating every corner of our tiny home. Bear crammed herself into a smaller and smaller space on the couch as the kittens scaled the back of it, clawed at the underside, sliding themselves along the floor on their backs and tumbled and jostled and poured themselves into everything.

One day I found the two dilute calicos playing by the front door. The closet was an endless source of intrigue for the kittens since there was no door to shut and mark the things inside off limits. When I found the kittens, they were investigating a pair of Morgan's shoes. One had climbed inside the left shoe and was sitting there like a picture when I saw her, paws resting on the top edge, head and shoulders emerging from the mouth of the shoe. It was adorable and I grabbed my camera to get a picture before I plucked the other kitten, the one who would be Cleo, from the lace front of the right shoe, where she was tackling with great glee the loose end of the shoelace, tiny needle claws grasping, needle teeth tearing.

Her body was so delicate, tiny bones beneath the kitten fluff, ribs no bigger than toothpicks encasing tiny heart and lungs. Her whole body fit in the palm of my hand, and I scooped her up to my chest, held her for a moment against my heart that was probably not much smaller than the kitten

The Comeback Cat

herself, and then she was climbing with Velcro claws out of my hand and up to my shoulder. She perched there momentarily, surveyed the room from the new vantage point, stretching her neck, standing on the tips of her toes, perhaps angling to leap from the precipice, fly through the air to land on one of her brothers turning somersaults on the couch.

But she stretched too far, misjudging the sturdiness of her perch, her foot slipped and the rest of her followed and she was falling. Down, down, the ceiling high above. It was one of those moments that seemed to sidestep time, each second stretching on and I felt like I was watching her fall for a long time before I knelt with my hand out to catch her. I don't know if she would have flipped around to land on her feet, the way cats do, or if she was too young yet to have that register as an ability, but maybe I shouldn't have interfered because when I caught her she slammed to a sudden stop, jolting her head, and she stared up at me with a dazed expression on her face for a moment before I placed her gently on the floor and watched her trot away.

I can't be sure, but I feel as though that was a turning point for Cleo, a catalyst for her increasingly strange behaviour over the years, the covert missions under the house, the random acts of destruction for the fun of it, the blank-eyed lingering stares at the ceiling, the body-stiffening, panicked flailing if I ever tried to pick her up higher than a couple of feet off the floor, the single-minded independence bordering on antisocialism that cemented her never-quite-fitting-in with her siblings and made her in to a cat nobody wanted.

The Comeback Cat

The early offer of homes for the kittens disappeared soon after they were made for various reasons, all sound. Mostly it was a matter of practicality setting in after the initial wash of sentimentality for a cute face and bundle of fur had passed. So we cast about to find families for the kittens, asking friends, posting notices on local neighbourhood boards.

A few months later, after the dust had settled, we were left with Chestnut and Cleo. Chestnut could have been re-homed a dozen times, but I wouldn't let him go always drawing attention to the other kittens, including Cleo. But people weren't interested and eventually we stopped looking.

So, Cleo was ours by default more than anything else, settling into her life of eccentricities as Chestnut became the cat I had always wanted, a cat who preferred a warm lap over a cushion on the couch, who purred at the drop of a hat, who loved to be picked up and hugged and carried about.

Cleo was happy to do her own thing, so we just let her get on with it, which probably helped shape her independent personality even more. We assumed she didn't need us, so we gave her space, so she took more space and we talked about her like some strange extraterrestrial living among us.

But Cleo's lack of neediness was one of the best things about her. While everyone else in our furry family clamoured for attention, Cleo flitted about the periphery and into the midst of the chaos, seemingly unaffected by all of it. She was the one animal I never had to worry about, she was never sick, never injured, never lost. She was dependably independent.

Nine years later I wonder if she is far more interesting and engaging than I gave her credit for, now that I am spending my days keeping tabs on her, talking to her a lot more, petting her and doting on her.

But armed with the insulin and the antibiotic, I imagine I become like a specter to Cleo, descending on her twice a day to jab her in the back of the neck and stuff a pill down her throat.

I feel like a turncoat kneeling beside her where she is folded into her box on the floor, petting her gently, uttering phrases like "Nice kitty," or "You're such a good girl." And then grabbing her head, forcing her mouth open with a finger from each hand pressed firmly against the hinge of her jaw and jamming a pill to the back of her throat with a third finger trying to avoid the mutinous tongue and the sharp, cutting teeth. And then I have to do it again immediately with another half pill.

The first few times I seem to take her by surprise enough that the whole thing is over before she really knows what happened. But she catches on quickly and starts fighting me off with her paws as I manhandle her face, poking my fingers at her jaw and into her mouth. Sometimes she manages to spit out the pill and I try again but the pill is now wet and sticky and dissolving into a white chalk on my fingers.

"Come on Cleo," I half beg. "Just work with me and it will be so much easier." But she can't help herself and really I can't complain because she doesn't scratch and she doesn't bite and I don't need a second pair of hands to help.

But we have had the cats since they were too tiny to be on their own and we handled them from day one, so now when I cut their nails they sit calmly on my lap as I take one paw at a time in hand and gently push out their claws, neatly clipping each one, clip, clip, clip. And when I've had to give medications, short of a few pills spit across the floor, they have been reasonably cooperative.

This reasonableness is not at all what I thought cats could be like. I have seared in my brain the ordeal my parents used to have to go through when dealing with the cats we had when I was growing up. Anything was a battle that always involved two adults – no children for fear of mauling – and an angry cat wrapped up in a towel like a sausage roll so only her head was free. The cat always gave forth horrible yowling protests and growls and hisses and gnashing of teeth, while usually my mom half-sat on her to hold her down and my dad fought through the angry bites to administer the pills.

Regardless, I am still upset about the whole thing and I dread pill times, 'twice a day after meals'. By day twelve it is becoming much more difficult. If it was just one pill, it might have been all right, but it is too much to ask Cleo to let me do this twice in a row. She sits in her box, hunkers down, screws up her face, wrenches her head left and right, pulling it free from my hands, flails at me with her paws and once or twice makes a protesting sound in her throat. We do not quite finish the course of medicine.

The Comeback Cat

Cleo, I notice, has been ripping the hair out of her front paws again. There is a square patch of red raw skin on the topside of each wrist. It's stress, I'm sure of it, brought on by the sudden onslaught of needles in the neck and fingers almost jammed down her throat. Who wouldn't be stressed?

"I can't keep doing this," I tell Morgan, pointing out her damaged feet. "Look what she's doing. It's way too stressful for her." Way too stressful for me too, my spirit is just about broken, waking every morning with a sinking feeling in my heart knowing I have to assault the cat once more.

We have a vet visit planned in a couple of days, so I weigh the pros and cons, finishing the course of medication versus everybody retaining some level of sanity, and decide to stop administering the pills.

Chapter 6

It is still mostly dark as we bundle ourselves out the door wrapped in winter garb, toques and mitts and heavy coats, squeak our way down the snowy path between trees in various states of health or decay towards the driveway. Our breath emerges as puffs of steam even as we settle into the car. The plastic carrier with Cleo inside sits heavily on my lap. I can feel a little pool of warmth in the center where her body heat transfers through the blanket inside and the hard, cold plastic.

It is December 22, the day after the shortest day of the year. Though, for weeks, we have already been bungling about in heavy grey light in the mornings and early evenings, where the snow lying cold and flat on the ground aids in illuminating the twilit hours.

Morgan in the driver's seat turns the key and the car, our 1981 diesel Volkswagen Rabbit, rumbles roughly to life in a miserable sort of way as though it would prefer to pull the covers back over its head and wait for the sun to arrive. He hands me a plate, two slices of toast with jam slide about on top and I imagine them to be like blocks of ice. His breakfast, snagged as he stumbled through the kitchen half awake, determined to stay in bed till the very last second.

I roll my eyes, but hold the plate above the carrier as Morgan puts the car in gear and we roll backwards down the driveway, rushing because we have waited till the very last second, and because we are rushing, the slight curve in the driveway is missed and we plough into the snow bank at the end where it meets the road, the wall of snow absorbing the back corner of the car, packing into the undercarriage.

"Oops," Morgan says with a laugh. Cleo meows and I close my eyes, breathe out heavily, a thousand words of frustration piling up at the back of my throat but I say nothing. "Well, the winch is set up," he says as he swings himself out of the car, annoyingly chipper. I sit for a moment in the cold car as Morgan trudges back up the driveway towards the 22-foot sailboat where it sits in a metal cradle, bundled against the cold and topped with snow. Attached to the cradle with a chain is Morgan's 1,000-pound hand winch, put there to move logs up the driveway to his portable bandsaw mill that is set up beside the driveway just down from the boat. We have hauled that winch up into the woods to move fallen trees and down to the road to unstick many a ditched vehicle. So, even in the frustration of the moment I can appreciate that the winch does not need to be moved in to position and anchored to a tree.

I get out of the car, leave the plate of toast on the driver's seat and place the cat carrier on the

The Comeback Cat

passenger seat, "I'll be right back," I say to Cleo, and head to the house as Morgan digs out straps and chain, begins to roll out the winch cable.

"I'm just going to call the vet," I say and follow the squeaking, snowy path back to the house. We are supposed to be at the vets' office when it opens that morning, getting Cleo in for the first appointment of the day, before she eats breakfast, before her shot of insulin. We have packed those things to take with us because we are supposed to leave Cleo there all day so the vet can measure her peak and trough insulin levels, get an idea of where she is at after having been on insulin for over a week, make some decisions about how to proceed.

The trough levels are measured first thing in the morning. We are told, at this point, the insulin is at its lowest level in the bloodstream and glucose is at its highest, exactly 12 hours since her last shot of insulin and her last meal when her body has been left to its own devices. In a diabetic cat this most likely means the pancreas has been unable to produce enough insulin to deal with the increasing concentration of glucose in the blood.

Cleo will then sit in a cage somewhere in the back of the vet clinic for half the day waiting until they pull her out again to test her levels at midday to get a peak reading when her glucose will be at its lowest point, right in the middle of her insulin injections: six hours after breakfast, six hours before supper. At this point the insulin should be at its peak level of activity in the body shuttling fuel in the form of glucose out of the bloodstream and into cells.

The Comeback Cat

The receptionist chuckles appreciatively when I tell her we are stuck in our driveway and we're running a bit late though we should be there soon. We are lucky that most of the people who work at the vet clinic live in the country and understand first hand these kinds of things.

I pull my boots on again, say goodbye to the dogs again as I slip out the door, and then quick march down the path, past the trees, back to the driveway where Morgan has hooked up the winch to the car and is waiting for me to get behind the wheel and try to drive out as he winches, the plate of toast now perched on the snow bank on the other side of the driveway.

"Hi Cleo," I say as I get in and adjust the seat. "Sorry about this."

I put the car in gear as the winch cable tightens, creaking and popping metal against metal. The engine revs, the wheels spin, the car doesn't move.

I get out and start shoveling the snow from behind the car, wedge myself between it and the snowbank, which is blue in the early morning light, and try to scoop snow away from the back tire. We try again with the winch cable illuminated in yellow by the car headlights and Morgan a dark figure at the edge of the light cranking the winch. I rev the car again as the metal creaks and groans, and then I get out and shovel some more.

The sky is lightening, shades of indigo and pink, as we finally turn off our dead-end road and head to the valley and the vet clinic. As we emerge from amongst the trees and come down the long sloping road from the mountain, the sun sends its first rays to peek above the near distant Nor'wester mountain range that half-circles the valley to the south-east.

Cleo meows forlornly from her kennel on my lap and I talk to her every few minutes over the rumble of the exhaust and the rattle of the car as it passes over dips and holes in the road.

I am undoing my seatbelt, opening the car door before it has barely stopped at the front door of the clinic. I shuffle out with the carrier and Morgan grabs the bag with her food and insulin and we tumble through the door into the warmth and light of the clinic.

The girl at the desk ushers us straight in to the exam room where the vet and vet tech are waiting for us and we get right to it, opening the carrier and letting Cleo free to clonk about the room as we discuss what's been going on.

"I stopped giving her the medication for her bladder infection," I confess and rush to explain. "She got most of it but it was getting so stressful she's started ripping the hair out of her paws. Look," I say, picking Cleo up off the floor and presenting her front paws with their pink, irritated patches, to the vet.

"Oh," she says, examining them with some concern. "We can give her an injection of the medication today if you want."

Morgan and I glance at each other, nod quickly in agreement. "That would be great," I say.

"The injected medication doesn't usually work as well as the pills," She explained further. "But since the pills have been stressing her out, we'll do the injection. We don't want her in distress."

And then she suggests that we don't leave her with them all day as planned. Stress, she tells us, will affect her glucose levels and they won't get an accurate reading.

"We can do the trough reading now and make another appointment for another day to do the peak reading," she explains. "But the best thing to do is home glucose testing, that will give us the most accurate readings."

"Oh?" I say.

"It's the same glucometer you use for humans," she says. "And there's a vein that runs along the edge of the ear, you prick just beside that to get the blood and then keep a record of her sugar levels."

Oh my god, I think, her ear? I've tried one of those before on my finger and it is not painless. Her ear? I take a moment and imagine the pandemonium, the clawing, the growling, the hissing, and biting.

My thoughts must have been written across my face because the vet laughs and says, "It's not as difficult as it sounds. It is actually quite easy with practice. There are videos online you can watch and we will show you how to do it."

"Okay," I say with a laugh as if it is no big deal. I do not add that Morgan is leaving town in two weeks and I will be on my own trying to manhandle the cat. This is a task I imagine must be performed with two people. As amiable as my cats are, I figure this will be the limit. I picture the sausage-rolled family cats of my youth, my parents working as a team, and imagine this is what we will have to do.

For now we make another appointment to return in a week at a more civilized hour to have Cleo's trough levels recorded. And then we pack up our things and head home.

Over the next week our days at home are much calmer since I am no longer stuffing pills down Cleo's throat. The fur on her paws seems to be growing back in and she spends most of her time sleeping in her box in the kitchen. We are home over Christmas, the quiet, cold days spent cutting firewood, visiting friends, eating lots. Our time is planned out around Cleo's insulin injections. We go to a neighbours' house for dinner but have to duck out early to get home for Cleo. We babysit our friends' kids one evening and Morgan slips out for an hour to dash home and give Cleo her insulin, returning in time to put the kids to bed. I am up early in the morning, before the sun most days, to give Cleo her injection. We fluctuate times by half hour increments. If we know we have an evening planned in town, we step her insulin and feeding times backwards over the course of a number of days so she can get her injection between 5:00 and 6:00 and we can go out without worrying. Of course that also means we have to get up early and make sure she gets her morning injection between 5:00 and 6:00; every 12 hours.

On December 29 we head back to the vet to have Cleo's peak numbers checked. It is midday; the sun is high in a blue sky making the air extra crisp to go with the starched, white perfection of the snow.

The Comeback Cat

Cleo has been sleeping off and on inside her cat carrier where we left it in the kitchen so I like to think it is not as traumatic when I put her in it this time and close the door, though I apologize again, "Sorry Cleo," as we step from the warmth of the house into the cold outdoors.

She resumes her complaints as we travel over the familiar road to the vet, those long drawn-out meows that sound like a sorrowful ballad. It is kind of funny and we joke with her on our way down the hill, pointing out the cows and horses we pass as if she might care.

At the vet clinic we sit in the waiting room with Cleo on the floor peering out from the depths of her carrier at the other animals coming and going before we are ushered in to the exam room.

We exchange pleasantries with the vet tech as I place the carrier on the floor and swing the door wide. Cleo lurches out, stumbles awkwardly, almost face-plants on the linoleum. I laugh at first, and point, thinking she has tripped over the threshold of the kennel, the lip that encircles the wire-cage door. But then she is flopping about in a desperate kind of way as though she has been thrown into a lake and can't swim. She flails at the floor unable to get her feet beneath her.

The laugh leaves my voice immediately. "What's wrong with her?" I say, wondering if her feet have fallen asleep. She is shaking them about like she is trying to restore feeling.

"That's not normal," says Morgan

"She was not doing that before," I say to the vet tech.

"I'll go get the vet," she says and hastily leaves the room, returning almost immediately with the vet in tow.

Cleo has stopped flopping about, but sits huddled on the floor, her back feet tucked under her, leaning awkwardly forward on her front legs that seem to bend beneath her weight as though they are made of rubber.

"It looks like peripheral neuropathy," says the vet. "It isn't common, but it does sometimes affect the front legs too." And she is looking at Cleo as though she has never seen this before.

My heart drops in my chest. For a moment I am speechless as I scramble through the tumbling thoughts in my head. Are you kidding me? How is this possible? I thought we were treating this thing. I thought we were at least going to stop its progression now that she's on insulin, if not reverse it. Suddenly this all seems more real, more serious, my view of remission shrinking to a very far point on the horizon. And then it dawns on me; the ripping out of her hair from her front paws perhaps was not from stress. Maybe her legs had been bothering her for some time.

"Let's see what her peak levels look like," said the vet in her upbeat manner, bringing us back to the reason for our visit. "We are going to use the clinic's glucometer today so you can see how it's done."

Right, I think, lifting Cleo from the floor onto the exam table, trying to get the rug back under my feet from where it had been whisked moments ago.

The Comeback Cat

The vet tech is the resident expert on using the glucometer. She has taught a number of people to do this and she explains the process to us before actually doing it. We watch as the vet holds Cleo in her arms and the vet tech clicks on an electric razor. The frenzied hum fills the room and I brace myself. This can't be good, I think, watching panic flash across Cleo's eyes; her ears go flat and her body tense. But the vet tech slips her finger beneath the thin edge of Cleo's grey ear and moves the razor gently across it and then turns it off.

Her hair is so thin on her ears anyway it seems a bit like overkill to me to use a razor, and why target the grey ear? I wonder. Her other ear is beige and the vein is easier to see. But the shaving, they explain, also makes it easier to collect the blood, so the hair does not wick it away in all directions.

Next, with a cotton ball held on the inside of Cleo's ear and the ear pulled taut across it, the vet tech pricked the spot beside the vein with a practiced hand and instantly a little globe of blood appeared on the edge of Cleo's ear. The aim, she explained, is to hit a capillary beside the vein and not the vein itself, which would bleed way too much and leave a bruise on the ear.

With the testing strip clicked into place on the meter, the vet tech then held it against the blood and took the reading with the meter. It was over before it had barely begun as Cleo continued to cling to the vet's shoulder and the vet tech held the cotton ball against the ear to stop the bleeding.

When Cleo is placed back down on the table, she heads straight for me where I stand on the other

The Comeback Cat

side and pushes her head in to my chest as if to hide. It is only the second time in her life that she gave any indication that she needed anyone but herself. The first was when we gave her away.

When Chestnut and Cleo were about eight months old, their sister came back to live with us. She was the other dilute calico in the litter and we had named her Broom Hilda before she went to live in her new home, but when her owner's circumstances changed, we took her back.

Broomie was an incredibly likeable cat. Originally when it seemed as though we were definitely going to end up with more than one cat, our second choice, after Chestnut, was Broom Hilda. She was engaging, sharp witted, clever and social, nothing like Cleo who seemed content to live in her own little world.

But we did not want to end up with three cats so when we had the opportunity to give Broom Hilda away we reluctantly took it. Five months later she was back with us, suddenly a stranger to Chestnut and Cleo even though the three of them had once been inseparable.

The day she returned, Chestnut was the happiest cat I've ever seen. Broomie hadn't been spayed yet and he would not stop following her around, even though she made it quite clear she thought he should go drop dead somewhere. Cleo was less than impressed to have another female in the house and growled, hissed and swatted at her any chance she had.

We made an appointment to have Broomie fixed within the next week and spent that time obsessively guarding the door against her mad-dash attempts to escape into the wild yonder. The last thing we needed was a bunch of kittens.

I awoke early one morning, the sky sporting just a hint of deep steel blue on one horizon as darkness seeped towards the other, and I had this strange feeling that someone was missing. I'm not sure how I knew, but I was compelled to get out of bed and do a quick head count.

Cleo sat up tall and owl-like in the living room, and in retrospect probably quite chuffed that somebody was going to get in trouble while Chestnut paced in the kitchen almost worriedly. Broom Hilda was nowhere to be found. It wasn't until my third pass through the kitchen that I noticed the screen on the half-open window above the sink was gone. The empty space yawned accusingly back at me and I leapt onto the counter and stuck my head out the window.

Seven feet down, the screen lay on the ground directly below at an angle, resting on the spring plants that had grown quickly against the sunny side of the house. I looked from left to right, but after the light from the kitchen, my eyes couldn't see very far in the dark grey of the morning.

I jumped back down to the kitchen floor, where Morgan now stood, bleary from sleep, wanting to know what happened. We grabbed flashlights and headed outside to track down the escapee.

My feet crunched on the gravel of the driveway that became a single-track road connecting all the houses in our community. I was sure I saw a white flash up ahead in the grey light. I trained my flashlight on it, but it was gone.

After searching fruitlessly, Morgan and I returned to the house with our flashlights turned off and half-heartedly calling for Broomie, knowing that even on an exceptional day cats will come only when they are good and ready.

I was just stepping through the door of our house when Morgan said, "There she is!" Broomie appeared at a run amidst the overgrown tangle of raspberry bushes that grew on the hill tumbling away from our square of deck down to the river. She tore up from the water, taking huge strides that made her seem as though she was flying across the ground. Her eyes flashed wildly and we could see hot on her tail was another cat. Broomie ran straight inside the house and we slammed the door behind her.

It was another month of Chestnut mooning over Broomie and Cleo casting dark, evil glances her way before we found her a new home. But during the search we decided to put Cleo back up for adoption as well so when the prospective new family contacted us about the cats we gave them the choice of either Broom Hilda or Cleo, offering a trial run of them keeping both cats over night and deciding which one they wanted.

It was the first time I realized I had actually become attached to Cleo and her eccentricities. That first night she was gone Chestnut wandered aimlessly around the house meowing mournfully and wondering where everyone went. I just felt horribly guilty, with butterflies in my stomach each time I thought about how I had betrayed Cleo.

The Comeback Cat

When the new family called the next day and said they would keep both cats because they didn't want to split up sisters, my heart sank and I felt like I had made a terrible mistake. "But Broom Hilda and Cleo hate each other," I said to Morgan, and listened to more sad yowling from lonely Chestnut.

Cleo lived with that family for two nights. The second day she was gone I couldn't think of anything else but her. I went to work feeling like I had lost my best friend and like I had ruined Chestnut's life. In my selfishness of wanting to make life easier with just one cat, I had casually thrown away a member of our family.

When I got home that day, convinced I was the worst person in the world, I talked to Morgan about it and he called the new family to ask if we could have Cleo back, giving an abbreviated version of the events that led to Broom Hilda returning to us, of Chestnut's loneliness and the obvious mistake we'd made by giving Cleo away.

The woman was agreeable to giving Cleo back, something I understood more when I later stood in her living room surveying the devastation of her previously lush and beautiful houseplants. But when Cleo saw me standing there, she ran at top speed across the room, meowing, and jumped into my arms. I scooped her up and she purred happily against my face. Clearly, she knew where she belonged and I popped her into the cat carrier and took her home.

I am reminded of that moment when standing at the vet with Cleo's head pushed into my chest. I run my hand down her back and tell her she's fine and I am newly determined to make her well again, even if it includes learning how to do home blood glucose testing, even if it means I will be doing it alone without an extra pair of hands, as Morgan is scheduled to leave town in the new year to work 1,700 kms away in Kingston.

Chapter 7

Home glucose testing seems like a really good idea, in theory. I nod and agree with the vet when she brings it up, that yes it is a good way to keep a close eye on changing blood sugar levels, to create a graph and a curve to track how Cleo reacts to the insulin. But then I kind of baulk at how casually it is mentioned as though we are not talking about cats, as though it is a completely reasonable thing to do.

I watch some videos online of people home testing their cats. It looks so easy. What kind of cats are these? I wonder. They just lie there casually on blankets without batting an eye while humans prick holes in their ears.

This will be the moment, I am suddenly sure, in the process of trying to extract blood from her ear, that Cleo will go over the edge, become like our family cats when I was growing up, those refined felines who turned completely psychotic at the mere suggestion of having their claws clipped, let alone the prospect of having pills rammed down their throats. There's no way, I thought, even though I watched the vet and vet tech perform the task on Cleo without any problems. But they always make things look easy.

If anyone were going to turn into a psychotic feline, I was sure, it would be Cleo. With her mysterious motives, her fastidious attention to personal space and overall less personable nature, Cleo is naturally suspicious of everyone. I am not entirely certain she won't tap into her inner demon and shred me to bits, but I am willing to try.

We price out a glucometer and the strips and lancets at a local pharmacy, explaining somewhat sheepishly that it's for our cat and we don't need anything fancy. The cost is prohibitive considering Morgan is just leaving town for a new job and I am between jobs and we're not even sure Cleo will let me do this thing at all.

We have a quick look online for a used machine that last week of December as Morgan packs for his trip. He will be driving to southern Ontario and staying with my family to try out a new job before we make a more permanent decision. The week is full of last minute things, of firewood, car maintenance, gathering supplies for a winter road trip, visiting with neighbours and just spending time together.

Plans of me going for the occasional visit have been shelved now because of Cleo's needs and we are unsure of how soon we will see each other again. We spend New Year's Eve together and then on January 2, 2015 Morgan drives away. I stand with the dogs at the end of the driveway, one hand firmly curled around Murdoch's collar, our car-chasing wonder dog, while waving with my other. Molly sits at attention by my side, a mildly bewildered expression on her face.

Morgan turns the corner at the stop sign and when I can no longer hear the rumble of the diesel engine, I release Murdoch and trek back up the driveway to the path through the trees and on to the house. The dogs skip behind me and then jostle for position at the door. Inside I throw another log on the woodstove, to the sound of crackles and pops, remove my coat and boots and then head to the kitchen and turn on the kettle for tea.

I settle in to man the phone and email for the next couple of days, updating my family and Morgan's during his trip since he is driving and it is winter and the weather can be unpredictable, the roads either perfectly clear or closed by blowing or drifting snow.

After Cleo was diagnosed with diabetes in December, I called my mom and dad to tell them. I don't remember the conversation exactly, but there would have been a lot of "oh no"s and "what now"s and "what next"s, because with a pack of animals in the house it seems like there's always something.

And there is. We usually don't get too far ahead of one crisis before another one pops up to take its place. Six months before Cleo started showing signs of diabetes, Chestnut had gone through his latest battle with urinary crystals, which had been triggered by us bringing Molly home a few months before that. Molly's arrival came just nine months after we were gutted by the loss of Bear who had spent the previous year valiantly living with cancer through endless vet visits, medications, and seizures.

The Comeback Cat

Before the cancer, there were cruciate ligaments and knee braces. There was a deteriorating Max, his backend and his wheelchair, and more bouts of urinary crystals for Chestnut. There was finding Murdoch on the side of the road and the ensuing battles to try and shape him in to something resembling a dog, and before that there was the disappearance of Quincy who wandered off in the woods one day and never returned. We scoured the countryside for months, taped notices to mailboxes, waited by the phone. But there was no sign of him.

So yes, there is always something and sometimes it works out and sometimes it doesn't.

When I tell my parents about home glucose testing, they agree that it is going to be nearly impossible given their experiences with cats over the years and the cost of the equipment would be a waste, so my dad, who uses a glucometer himself, tells me he is getting a new machine and will send me his old one with some lancets and strips.

I wait excitedly for the package to arrive, checking the mailbox almost every day, making the trek to the corner with my key to unlock the little metal door on the face of the superbox. It comes the second week of January; I swing open the door to find the brown cardboard box crouched expectantly in the darkness, bursting with possibility. I fumble it into the light and hurry home with it on the passenger seat of the car.

At the kitchen table I rip open the box and spill out the contents. The glucometer and lancing device are packaged back in the original box looking brand new, classic dad. There are two rattling

The Comeback Cat

canisters of test strips and a clear pill bottle repurposed to house a bundle of lancets, which are little metal pins encased in molded white plastic for being inserted into the lancing device. I pull out the instructions for the machine and the lancing device, a small white and blue plastic tool ergonomically designed to fit in your hand, curving over curled fingers with a big square button on top to be depressed by your thumb that releases the lancet at speed with a spring-loaded click.

I read through the instructions and then click a lancet into place. I turn on the glucometer, insert a small, white test strip and when the machine recognizes it, it beeps to life. I set it down on the table and hold the lancing device against the side of my index finger. I take a breath, hesitate, because I've done this before and I know it hurts, and then I press the button. There's a click and a sharp sting, like the sting of a wasp, and a slow swirl of blood forms a small globe on the side of my finger. Holding the glucometer I touch the test strip to the blood, watch as it is sucked up as if by a straw, and wait for the meter to flash the number indicating my blood sugar level.

"Okay," I say, turning to where Cleo lies ensconced in her box. "It works." And I pop out the used lancet, put a fresh one in the machine, grab the glucometer, strips, and a few cotton balls from the bathroom and then drop down beside her box, arrange the things I need beside me.

I pet her for a minute and worry about hurting her. Cat's ears are so papery thin and a legitimate concern I have read while looking for any information I could find about home glucose testing, is poking a hole with the lancet straight through the ear.

But then there is that little notch in the side of her ear, I think and run my finger over it. That's where Chestnut bit her years ago a little too exuberantly in an especially rough game of war. Cleo appeared on my lap that day with a tiny flap of skin hanging from the edge of her ear that eventually hardened and fell off. She didn't seem too concerned about it, so perhaps the ears are not as sensitive as I thought. Or Cleo is just that tough.

I rub her ears gently between my fingers to warm them up and get the blood flowing. It is recommended to use a warm washcloth inside a plastic bag, but I imagine that might be a bit intimidating for her, so I just use my fingers and then put my lips against the beige ear, the target ear, feeling the coolness of her skin against mine, breathing a few puffs of warm breath against its papery thin edge as you would breathe on the lens of a pair of sunglasses to polish away water spots.

Cleo seems relaxed and happy even as Chestnut helpfully sticks his nose in her face and bumps my elbow with his head, "Why are you paying so much attention to her?" he seems to want to know.

"What are you doing? What is this? What's going on here?" he adds as he paws at the glucometer lying at the ready beside me on the floor and tries to steal the cotton balls.

"Chestnut go away," I say, giving him a shove and trying to reclaim the glucometer as he swats my hand. I force myself to remain calm as he circles around, bumps my other elbow. I don't want Cleo to feel my nervousness, which is being compounded by my annoyance at Chestnut's pushiness. But so far she seems remarkably unflappable, barely giving Chestnut a glance through half-closed eyes.

I shove Chestnut away again and slip a cotton ball against the inside edge of Cleo's ear, pull the ear taut against it as though it is nothing out of the ordinary. Cleo doesn't seem too bothered besides a vague expression of curiosity that crosses her face. I take a deep breath, place the lancing device just beside the thin red vein that parallels the edge of her ear millimeters away, and press the button.

Inside the little device with the blue top, the lancet is let loose with a spring and a click and barely a reaction from Cleo. But when I pull it away from her ear, turning to pick up the glucometer, there is nothing. No blood, no obvious puncture mark. So I reset the lancet and try again, ear pulled taut against the cotton ball, lancing device resting against her ear just to the right of the red vein, button pushed with a spring and a click. Nothing.

I try again, this time resetting the depth of the lancet. With my concern about sending the needle-sharp point straight through her ear I had initially adjusted it to the shallowest setting. I am confident it will work this time as I go through the steps again. But again there is nothing.

Now I am getting frustrated and no longer trying to pretend I am not. Cleo is getting annoyed, having had enough of me manhandling her ear,

The Comeback Cat

pulling it this way, pushing it flat. She looks up at me from beneath a stormy brow.

"Why isn't this working?" I say to the room and reset the lancet and fire it into the air. But the lancet springs out so fast and back again I couldn't tell how far out it came. It had worked on my finger so it should work on her ear.

At the vet's office when they were demonstrating how to do this they were out of lancets so they used some other pointed tool and free handed the prick. On the floor in my kitchen with Chestnut swiping more cotton balls and Cleo sinking down farther into her box, I pulled the cap off the lancing device and examined the metal lancet within, the slight bend in the metal tapering down to the finest, tiniest point and I wondered if I could free hand this myself.

It is one thing to put a plastic, not unfriendly looking device against your skin, or your cat's ear, push a button and magically have a drop of blood on the skin when you pull the device away, it is quite another to purposely stick someone with a pin hard enough to do the same thing. How much pressure should I use? How deep should I go?

I steel myself, petting Cleo again, starting over. I put the cotton ball in place, line up the now exposed lancet near the vein in her ear and give it a quick jab at her skin. She flinches at that, but there is no obliging bubble of blood. I try again and again. Harder this time, faster that time, then slower, until I have a line of dots on her ear which is getting red, and an angry cat meowing harshly each time I poke her and starting to squirm.

The Comeback Cat

"What the hell?" I say in frustration and try again, this time getting a tiny smear of blood. I know it isn't enough for the glucometer to get a reading, but it is all I have and I try anyway, placing the strip attached to the machine against the meager trickle of blood.

I watch as the strip sucks up what is there, quietly willing it to be enough, "come on, come on." But it only fills half the channel in the strip, petering out well before it reaches the meter.

"Oh, come on," I say, many decibels louder as the machine beeps and flashes an error message in orange on the screen. I grumble loudly as I snatch up all the paraphernalia from the floor, Cleo glares in to her box and Chestnut circles at a distance. I turn and drop everything on the table with a loud clatter and stomp off to walk the dogs.

I take Murdoch and Molly on our usual trail through the bush, crisp snow crunching under my boots as the dogs run ahead along the looping path around the trees. I follow, try to walk off my failed attempts at doing this blood-testing thing. Try to figure out what I did wrong, what I can do differently next time.

And yet I am struck by Cleo's agreeableness during the entire process, the pulling and tugging of her ear, the poking her repeatedly with the wasp-like stinger. How did she not turn and bite me?

Cleo has always been a tough cat, a survivor, a pusher of boundaries. She has not overcome insurmountable odds to prevail and thrive, nothing as dramatic as that. She has just never shied away from perceived danger, a trait that is at once admirable and also a little concerning.

Her lack of fear towards the dogs, in particular Murdoch, who could, if they wanted to, kill her with one snap of the jaws have led Morgan and I to discuss what would happen if she ever stumbled upon a pack of wolves out in the woods. We imagined she would trill with excitement, skip into their midst and announce herself with something like a cheery, "Hi! I'm Cleo. I love dogs," and expect to be welcomed into their family without a second thought, never mind the gobs of drool dripping from razor sharp teeth.

Cleo's refusal to view dogs as any sort of potential threat began when the cats were tiny, inexperienced kittens living in a box in our home. That first day they lived with us I'm sure they imprinted on Bear, even though she dismissed the lot of them after a meticulous probe with her nose.

The minute the kittens had any freedom they clung to Bear, following her around, erasing fears, as Bear tried to first ignore them and then outrun them. Outside on the lawn the kittens scrambled across the grass, great big strides with their little bodies, traipsing along behind the big Black Lab, a little fuzzy mob of determination, while Bear bobbed and weaved in a vain attempt to lose them, just about tripping over herself trying to get away from the tiny terrors. We teased Bear relentlessly about the kittens thinking she was their mother.

Perhaps they identified Bear as closer to being like them than humans were. It caused Cleo at least to lose her fear of dogs. Chestnut only ever loved Bear.

The Comeback Cat

Any other dog who came near over the years was treated with great suspicion and disdain and inevitably caused Chestnut to suffer through another bout of urinary crystals. But Cleo has been determined to make friends with every dog we've had.

Max was an easy one, he was already a senior when he came to live with us, did not seem to have anything to prove and was happy just to have a warm, dry place indoors to sleep away from weather and swarms of bloodsucking bugs that had left his ears thickened and scarred from endless bites. He had spent a good chunk of his life living outdoors in all weather, in clattering rainstorms and the sharp-edged snap of winter that encased the floor of his doghouse in ice, which later became a small lake during the spring melt.

He was not remotely bothered by the cats and as such Cleo did not seem terribly intrigued by him other than to note there was another dog in the house. I imagine their interactions were more polite exchanges punctuated by dignified nods. "Cleo," Max would nod. "Max," she would nod back as she wandered past his bed of bunched up blankets.

Murdoch, I think, became Cleo's special project. Whether she saw something in him with which she identified, that loner vibe, the outsider, one of the unwanted, or just found him more entertaining than the rest of the family, I don't know. But wherever Murdoch was, Cleo wasn't too far away, finding creative ways to insert herself in to his life, sitting in front of his rattling, clanging kennel, popping randomly out from under the couch, sitting on top of his kennel and surveying him from above, using the woodstove as a shield as she slunk between it and the wall to make a beeline either for the window or the stairs.

Sometimes she would even purposely slow down in her attempts to escape his space, tiptoeing around the shoes left haphazardly beside the front door, casting sideways glances his way, waiting for him to notice so he would snarl or pounce or both and she could run for her life, covered in slobber, as if it were a great game.

When our most recent addition, Molly, the King Shepherd who was not used to cats, came to live with us we were worried about the dynamic of once again introducing a new dog to the family and were only half joking when we insisted if it was going to work it would be up to Cleo. Which it was. As Chestnut suffered another round of crystals, Cleo confronted the new dog with a sharp, claw-laden swat to the nose.

Cleo has bridged the gap in our home time and again between canine and feline. Perhaps our comparisons of Cleo to a scientist studying the curious interactions of humans and canines or to a space alien not quite getting the hang of disguising herself as an earthling feline have been wrong. Perhaps she is more of a peacenik deep down, determined to have us all just get along. Which could explain her astounding agreeableness when it comes to glucose testing.

I let a day go by after my first botched attempt to check Cleo's sugar levels. It is early afternoon when I gather up the supplies from where I

The Comeback Cat

left them on the kitchen table and find Cleo molded into the beanbag chair in the living room.

Besides her box, the beanbag chair has become Cleo's other favourite place to sleep. Its malleable form is perfect for her with the limited use of her legs. She doesn't have to jump up on anything. She just steps onto the edge and the tiny Styrofoam balls inside rustle and shift into a perfect little pocket just her size only inches off the floor. It sits near our pellet stove, which I light in the mornings and evenings to take the chill out of the air. The stove creates a zone of warmth that conveniently encompasses the beanbag chair and, by extension, Cleo.

On clear sunny days, even when it's cold outside, we do get warmth coming in at the windows and long yellow squares of light painted across the hardwood floor, so the pellet stove is usually off during the middle of the day. It is off today when I find Cleo sleeping in the quiet of the second floor of our house.

"Hi Cleo," I whisper as I sit down on the floor in front of her and set beside me the glucometer, lancing device with lancet in place and cotton balls. Chestnut helpfully arrives on cue as I start scratching the top of Cleo's head and then rubbing her cold ears as I did before. Chestnut pokes a white-tipped paw at the cotton balls and I push him away but he creeps back and bats at the glucometer. I move the machine to the other side of my body as I hear the lancing device go skittering across the floor.

"Chestnut," I say with a bit of a growl as I get up and retrieve it from below the windowsill. I sit down again with everything huddled in front of me in the space between the beanbag chair and my crossed legs. Chestnut circles the chair, pushes his face into Cleo's as I continue to warm her ears.

With the cotton ball in place on the inside edge of her ear, I take a deep breath, release it, try to relax, as I bring the unsheathed lancet to rest just beside the red vein snaking along parallel to the ear's edge. I pull the ear taut against the cotton ball, take aim with the lancet and give the skin a quick poke. I leave behind a dot, a tiny impression, on her ear, but there is no blood. I take another breath and try again, this time a little harder, and this time there is blood, not a lot but more than the last time I tried.

"Okay, hang on Cleo," I say, trying to remain calm as I fumble with the glucometer and the strip. I hold the strip to the dot of blood and watch it slowly creep up the tiny channel to the meter.

"Come on, come on," I quietly cheer it on. There seems to be just enough blood, but something goes wrong and another error message flashes orange across the screen of the machine.

"What the ...?! Come on!" I half shout into the room. Chestnut slinks away and Cleo flicks a glance in my direction before half-closing her green eyes and giving a slight wiggle of her shoulders to sink more comfortably into the chair.

I push myself up from the floor and stomp off down the stairs to get another strip because in my confidence I had only brought one with me. I mumble all the way down to the kitchen, annoyed with myself because here I am given a cat who couldn't be more accommodating and each time I do this incorrectly I imagine she will quickly lose patience with me and I will have lost my opportunity.

"Cleo, I'm so sorry," I say when I have returned and am sitting again in front of her with all the bits and pieces at hand, including an entire canister of test strips. I start over as though the previous attempt never happened, warming her now reddened ear with my fingers.

This time I poke hard and fast with the lancet. Cleo meows angrily as a perfect globe of dark red blood blooms on the edge of her ear. I clamp my hand on her head to hold her still, "Just wait," I say in a pleading voice as I grab the glucometer. This time the blood sucks up the channel like liquid in a straw. It is quick and over in an instant.

"Good girl Cleo!" I say, elated and giddy as I hold the cotton ball firmly against Cleo's ear to stop the bleeding and plant a kiss on the top of her head. She seems slightly bewildered, swinging quickly from annoyance to contentment at being lavished with praise.

The number flashes on the screen of the glucometer with a beep: 17 mmol/L. Not bad, I think, comparatively speaking. It is lower than the numbers we saw at the vet, but it still seems really high to me even though the information sheet written out by the vet claims our target range for Cleo is anywhere between 5.5 – 16.7 mmol/L. So, we're close.

I return all the glucose testing equipment to the kitchen table, where it will stay for the next three months, at hand and ready. I record the numbers in the memo section at the back of an outdated day planner full of photographs of various German

Shepherds doing adorable things. It is in this book I plan to keep track of all Cleo's insulin dosages, food amounts, and glucose readings.

I leave the pen between the pages when I close the book with a satisfied sigh. This might work, I think and feel relieved for a little while. But even though it finally went well and I got my first reading and Cleo didn't go on the attack, even though I know that practice makes perfect, I don't attempt another test for four days.

Chapter 8

It is the day after our first successful home glucose test and Cleo and I are in the car again driving down the mountain to the vet's office. She sits in her carrier on the passenger seat squeaking out half-articulate protests, trying in vain to be all forlorn but her voice, diminished by the disease, sounds like it is coming to me over a great distance through static. I try to blast heat through the vents but the cold of the crystal clear day comes off the windows in waves and when I talk to Cleo, my breath billows out in great puffs of steam. Outside, the trees seem frozen in place with no wind to create any movement across the landscape.

It will be a quick visit today so I leave the car running, concerned that the aging diesel engine won't want to start again in the cold. When I step through the door of the clinic, Cleo is quickly whisked away to have blood drawn and is returned with a bandage on her leg, lauded again for her good behaviour, "For a Calico," they always say.

The Comeback Cat

Cleo is having her fructosamine levels tested today. Fructosamine testing, I am told, gives an overview of average blood glucose concentrations in the body during the previous two to three weeks and it is not affected by external factors like stress so it is supposed to give a more accurate overview of how well the injected insulin is working in her system.

Cleo has been on insulin for just over a month, 2.5 units every 12 hours. The fructosamine test will hopefully give us a good picture of what her body is doing and the vet can decide if the amount of insulin Cleo is receiving is appropriate.

I tell the vet I have started home testing and she encourages me to do it as often as I can so we can chart the numbers and make decisions about any changes in insulin dose.

"When you've collected a few days worth of numbers, email them to me and we can create a blood glucose curve," she said. "But don't make any changes to her insulin without talking to me first."

"Of course," I say, not wanting to play around with Cleo's life. We were told from day one the biggest concern for a diabetic cat is if they become hypoglycemic, when their blood sugar drops so low their bodies can't function, a condition that can lead to the cat falling into a coma, experiencing seizures and even causing death.

One of the major causes of plummeting sugar levels is too much insulin injected into the system. It is all a very fine balancing act we were told right from the beginning, between insulin injections and food intake. The concern is so great, the vet explained, that the rule of thumb is to actually keep a cat slightly hyperglycemic in order to avoid the potentially fatal opposite end of the scale.

The vet calls me at home later with the results of the fructosamine test.

"It's not bad," she says. "Her number is 409 which is in the fair range." So she is just a hair outside the good range which is anywhere between 300-400. Normal is considered anything less than 300. Still, the vet decides to up Cleo's insulin by half a unit, bringing her to 3 units every 12 hours.

It is another three days before I test Cleo's blood glucose again. My reasoning for waiting is to lessen Cleo's stress since she just went to the vet again, but I am also still unsure about my ability to do it, so I talk myself out of it, make excuses.

It is January 19th when I wander down the stairs in the morning and find Cleo in her box in the kitchen and by the yellow light of the bulb hanging above the stairs to the entryway, I take a morning reading, a trough level. I have to make a couple of attempts before I get enough blood, but I do it without getting frustrated and Cleo lies there calmly and lets me do it. I record a glucose level of 20.3.

A couple of days later I do another morning test: 21.2. I spend the next few weeks testing on random days, alternating between morning and midday, troughs and peaks. I know I should ideally be testing at least twice a day, keeping track of her daily peaks and troughs, but I don't because it rarely goes smoothly and every time I do a test I feel like she and I both deserve a day off, or sometimes more.

I find Cleo either in her box in the kitchen or snugged into the beanbag chair in the living room and

I'm always surprised that she doesn't try to get up and leave when she sees me coming with all the blood testing paraphernalia. But her patience with me allows me to approach calmly and take my time through the process.

I never bothered trying to use the lancing device in its intended way after that first day when it wouldn't prick Cleo's ear. It had caused way too much stress, so I continued free-handing it, using the device as a handle and taking aim with the super-sharp lance just to the side of her vein. Mostly I had to poke her ear two or three times before getting the blood I needed to test, leaving her ear red and sore looking.

Sometimes it worked right away and once or twice I nicked the vein bringing out swirls of bright red blood in quantities enough to do five tests at once. It happened one time when she was sleeping on the couch and it must have hurt because she shook her head, red splatters hitting the cushions and blankets before I could mop up the blood from her ear.

I am also not encouraged to test more frequently because the numbers are so consistently high. I reason it is unfair to force this trauma on the cat to find out what I already know.

But, when I have collected a decent amount of numbers to get some kind of picture, I email them to the vet, express my concern that they are staying quite high and ask if we should be giving Cleo more insulin because it seems like the amount she's getting now isn't doing enough. The vet tries to reassure me the numbers aren't terrible and tells me to continue

The Comeback Cat

with 3 units of insulin until we do another fructosamine test mid-February.

I am left at once deflated and anxious. I feel like there must be more I can do. There is an overwhelming sense of loss of control, of watching a car crash in slow motion. I sit and wait and stare at Cleo, trying to see through her skin to her insides and what is going on in there.

I get a lot of advice from well-meaning people to be prepared because I might just have to face the fact that she can't be fixed, that maybe she should be put down. And I try to explain to those who don't see her every day that despite her sudden physical limitations, she seems happy. Her eyes are bright, her appetite is great, her bodily functions are working normally. She talks to me sometimes with that squeaky half-meow she has now and she and I are more connected than we have ever been. To me there is still hope.

It is not the first time I have felt helpless in the face of something beyond my control affecting the lives of my animals. There was Bear and her cancer, Max and his degenerative mylopathy, Quincy, with first his abscess and then his disappearance, and there were the kittens all those years ago when I thought they had been handed an imminent death sentence.

There was a time, about a month before the kittens were going to be ready for adoption, when we thought they all might have Feline Immunodeficiency Virus (FIV), something I knew nothing about. I was sure they were all going to die within weeks of each other. It all started with the standard calico.

The Comeback Cat

We were up early one morning. It was still dark out, and I opened the box to check on the kittens before going back to bed. The pile of furry bodies sprang to life with the first slants of light slicing in from the living room lamp. Amidst the flurry of tiny ears, busy legs, and fuzzy tails, I saw one motionless body left lying at the bottom of the box.

I picked her up gently in my hands, the little black and brown calico. She was breathing, but her eyes were closed. It was strange to feel her small, warm weight in my hand, different from the usual wriggling energy, the constant motion even in stillness that defines a kitten's body.

I thought, in their desire to be in contact with one another, to sleep in a heap like they always did, the group didn't notice their sister had begun to suffocate where she lay, stuck at the bottom of the pile.

The other kittens faded into the background of our living room as I curled myself into a corner of the couch, cradling her tiny body carefully in my hands. I stroked her head with the tip of my finger and whispered to her, "Please don't die."

We decided she must have aspirated some of the formula we fed them. Morgan shook his head sadly, not wanting to voice the thought that I read clearly in his face, that she wasn't going to make it.

Slowly though, over the next hour, she seemed to recover. Her eyes opened to slits at first, then she held up her head, looking around as though she'd just awaken from a faint.

Later that day she announced her recovery by scaling Morgan's brown recliner. Her barely-there needle-point claws propelled her to the top where she stood triumphantly, looking way down to where her siblings cavorted on the floor, and we named her Joan, after the warrior spirit of Joan of Arc.

Her recovery was short lived. It wasn't long before I once again found her lying motionless and flat at the bottom of the box when the commotion and cat hair had settled. I lifted her warm, limp body from where it lay amidst folds of blanket and sat with her again, straining at first to feel if she was breathing. It was so shallow. This time, she didn't respond. We took her to the vet that afternoon, a different clinic than Cleo would go to years later for her diabetes.

It's unfortunate, but the woman we saw was clearly not a fan of cats. She looked down her nose at our kitten and advised us to have all six of them euthanized. Then added, blank-faced, we should box the lot up and take them back to the Humane Society where Morgan had picked them up. That's what she would do. They were not our problem. We shook our heads. We wouldn't do either of those things. The kittens were our problem, a problem that became bigger as she told us more.

Without trying to hide the fact she thought we were wasting her time, the vet explained the kittens most likely all had FIV (similar to HIV in humans). It's a condition many, if not all, strays have. With useless immune systems, she said if any of them so much as caught a chill, they wouldn't survive.

She reluctantly gave us some antibiotics for Joan and we left the office in silence. Our drive home was filled with unspoken questions and concerns. The car burst at the seams with them. A mild panic

The Comeback Cat

began to weave its way through me as I replayed the vet's dire predictions in my head. The way she described it, I expected the kittens to drop dead at any minute.

"We're not putting them down," I finally said to Morgan, breaking the silence. "If they're all going to die in a few months anyway we'll keep them and give them a good life even if it is short."

Morgan agreed and when we got home we named the last three kittens who had not yet been named. There was already Dr. Evil and Mini Me of course, and there was Joan.

We quickly named one of the dilute calicos Broom Hilda because she was fascinated with the broom, which plied the floor of our little house multiple times a day to keep on top of all the kitten and dog hair that peppered every flat surface and clung to the furniture. Broomie, as we affectionately called her, would leap out from hiding spots to confront the broom as it swept by, sometimes riding the bristles from one side of the room to the other.

At the time Chestnut, with his swirly beige fur, reminded me of a creamy hazelnut coffee, but since I'm not a coffee drinker and Hazel didn't seem like the right name for him, I eventually decided to name him after the Chestnut Canoe Company. Morgan and I are both canoeists and one of Morgan's heroes, Bill Mason, always paddled a Chestnut. Partly I thought naming him after something Morgan really cared about would give Morgan a connection to this kitten with which I had already bonded.

Cleo, short for Cleopatra, was named for her good looks. But if we had thought long and hard about it, hadn't panicked because we thought the kittens had only weeks to live, we might have come up with something more interesting, perhaps even more fitting. It's not like she wasn't quirky from the beginning.

But I did wonder not too long after our second visit to the vet if perhaps we sealed Joan's fate by naming her after Joan of Arc, the doomed warrior who would die young. She never did recover from her state of lethargy, no response to the medication she was given. A few days later we were back at the vet with Joan purring quietly, head wobbling, unsteady on her feet.

"It's something neurological," we were told. "We can't do anything for her."

She was euthanized that day and we took her home in a shoebox to bury her on the edge of the woods behind our house.

I steeled myself then, thinking about the next few months and how we would have to repeat this day another five times as the kittens each succumbed. But then about a week later we found out from a friend that she knew someone who had a cat with FIV that lived to be 13 years old.

Oh. Well. That changed things.

We did not want to end up with five cats for the next ten, fifteen, maybe even 20 years. Morgan didn't even want one cat and I was only interested in keeping Chestnut because he was the cat I had always wanted, the posable cat who purred at the drop of a hat and melted into laps. So the scramble began again to find homes. The two orange cats found families very quickly, everyone falling in love with the colour of their fur. Broom Hilda took a little longer and by the time there was just Chestnut and Cleo we had mostly given up.

Pressed now to think of a different name for Cleo, my mind goes blank. She is Cleo. She has been Cleo for 10 years. But it is a forgettable name, a cat name. Sometimes I wish we had thought of something better. However, even as we stopped struggling to find her a home and toyed with the idea of two cats instead of one, we still weren't convinced she would be ours forever, so the name Cleo as far as we were concerned was a placeholder, like the others.

But Cleo is far more than just a pretty face. You can tell just by looking at her calm, quiet exterior there is much happening behind those piercing eyes. Even now in her diminished physical capacity she sits on the stairs or silently in the corner of a room just taking everything in. Nothing escapes her gaze. She is like an owl in a tree, watching.

She always reacted instantly to a flash of light, sun glinting off a shiny surface projected on the ceiling or the wall or the floor, a knife turned just so on a plate, a cell phone angled away from the window. Cleo was on the reflection in an instant, head snapping in that direction, eyes locked on, ready to flick left or right depending on where the light went next, ready to launch a quick reflex attack. That concentrated energy always defined Cleo.

Meanwhile Chestnut became more and more relaxed, indifferent almost. He would saunter in to a room, flick a glance at a curious light flashed on the wall and look away, uninterested. Not willing to waste the energy needed to try and catch, contain,

The Comeback Cat

maybe ingest this strange light. Once was enough for him and he glided by, shoulder blades rising and falling with each stride, that lazy swagger of a lion.

Their personalities were never more glaringly different than when we brought home a laser pen that was supposed to be a fun, engaging toy.

The red pinpoint on the floor seemed to vibrate even as we held the laser pen steady. It was one of those lights that splits in two or disappears if you look at it too long and when you moved it across a smooth surface it left a barely perceptible trail, almost as if time had been slowed down and then sped up again.

We introduced the laser pen to Chestnut and Cleo when they were not yet a year old. It was fun at first with the cats appearing like magic in the kitchen when we turned it on, dashing across the floor, lunging and swiping and trying to capture it under a paw. They shouldered each other out of the way, collided soundlessly like a couple of clouds sailing across the sky, little claws clicking against the linoleum, scrabbling at the wall. And then the red dot would stop and rest for a moment and the cats would sit and stare, collecting themselves silently, readying their muscles in motionless bodies for that explosive pounce to try and catch it out.

After a while Chestnut would get bored. We could tell he was losing interest when he lay down on his side, stretched his body straight out, reaching over his head and then making one last final attempt at a sneak attack from this prone position before half-closing his amber eyes and swishing his tail and leaving the room.

The Comeback Cat

But Cleo was a different story. She became obsessed. Cleo could not just walk away from the red dot. It became her mission in life to capture it, to understand what it was. She acted like it haunted her dreams. I believe she spent every waking moment thinking about it, planning her next attack, always waiting, waiting for it to appear again.

It wasn't good enough to have stamped it out with her little white paw when she lifted her foot to find the dot had vanished because we had turned it off and congratulated her, "You got it Cleo! Good kitty." She would look frantically around herself, 'Where'd it go? It was right here. I had it!'

If we made the dot slide under the fridge to not reappear she would sit in front of the appliance, legs tucked up underneath her, for hours just waiting for it to pop out again. When she finally gave up on her vigil, I knew she was still thinking about it. No matter what else was going on in the house part of her brain was still focused on the red dot.

The laser pen was attached to a key chain we kept in a drawer of an old desk in our kitchen. Cleo quickly associated the jingling sound of the key chain with the red dot. When her obsession was at its worst, you would just have to bump the laser pointer in the drawer when looking for something else and Cleo would come running in a panic, even jolting out of a deep sleep, skidding to a halt in the middle of the kitchen, head snapping this way and that, eyes wide and scanning every square inch of the floor. It was the same thing every time we grabbed the car keys off the shelf at the front door, she would come running, a crazed look, in her eyes, 'Where is it? Where is it?!'

So we gave the laser pen away. It took time, but Cleo eventually let it go, although I know if it showed up again tomorrow, nine years later, it would all be right there at the front of her brain. Unsettled scores and all that.

But how frustrated she would be if it did show up now, I think, with the effort she has to put in to just moving a few feet across the floor at a time. I can't imagine watching her trying to catch that little red dot with her uncoordinated limbs, her paddling and flopping.

And then the added insult as Chestnut glides by ignoring the red dot he could so easily chase and hunt to exhaustion. Cleo never had Chestnut's finesse in movement. She never moved like a lion. She never had that languorous, liquid stride of a wild cat. But she did always walk with great purpose. She marched or ran or leaped.

While Chestnut has always flowed into a room almost majestically, Cleo was more militant. She arrived. She approached everything with tenacity, which makes her immobility now so much more difficult to watch.

Chapter 9

I am sitting in the living room, curled on the couch by the window reading a book when I hear the familiar thump, clonk, pause of Cleo making her way up the carpeted stairs from the kitchen below. When she finally appears in the living room, she lies down on the hardwood floor and casts her bright green eyes around the room.

"Hi Cleo," I say and wait to see if she will want me to lift her up on to the couch to sit beside me or if she will paddle her way across the floor to flop into the little well she has created at the edge of the beanbag chair.

When Cleo pushes herself up from the floor, she turns towards the steep wooden stairs to the bedroom. I watch as she hauls herself up one step at a time, stopping on each stair to contemplate the next. She makes it about half way until she gets to the tiny step cut in the shape of a triangle to aid in the turn of the staircase. She rests her front paws on that step and seems to calculate its size as she lurches forward a bit and then back and then forward again before seeming

The Comeback Cat

to decide it is too small and cramped for her untrustworthy body. My heart drops as she turns around and thumps down the three steps back to the living room and flops across the floor to the beanbag chair, her face set in expressionless determination.

I imagine she is crushed, walking away as if nonplussed to save face, as if she didn't really want to go to the bedroom anyway. I imagine her disappointment, her sadness, and I know I am projecting all of my feelings on to her. She is a cat. They are far more adaptable than humans. Does she feel frustration at not being able to move like she used to, not being able to do all those graceful cat things, not being able to dash up the stairs two at a time? She doesn't seem concerned as she steps onto the edge of the beanbag chair, settles in to the rustle of a thousand Styrofoam balls shifting beneath her weight. I know she will stay there for most of the day.

Some days Cleo doesn't bother with the stairs at all, preferring to remain in the kitchen curled up in her box or folded into the cat carrier with her chin resting on the edge, keeping an eye on comings and goings.

She is definitely not getting any better, but I don't think she is deteriorating either until Morgan comes home for a visit after a month and a half away, takes one look at her and says, "She's way worse."

"Really?" I ask somewhat skeptically even though I am aware that I have been with her every day while Morgan is looking at her with fresh eyes.

The Comeback Cat

"Yeah. Her legs are way worse. I can't even watch that," he says, turning away, wincing as if it is indeed painful to watch.

'But look at her,' I want to say. 'Sure, her legs aren't working right but she's still Cleo, look at her bright eyes, her desire for social interaction, her never-ending interest in food.'

I had been the only person to see Cleo in a month and had spent a lot of time on the phone trying to convince people we were a long way from the dreaded conversation about euthanasia and if only they could see her. I had hoped for a more positive reaction when Morgan came home, some indication that we were moving in the right direction.

I only allow myself to half believe him. Cleo's numbers have been fairly steady after all, steadily high, but steady none-the-less, and the vet had been confident after the fructosamine test results a month earlier listed her as fair. Apparently her condition could be a lot worse than it is.

But that doesn't make it any easier to watch her struggle every day, to see her glucose levels still hovering around the 20 mmol/L mark, to continue the endless cycle of insulin every 12 hours and those hopeful moments of pricking her ear and thinking today will be the day something changes.

We have to cancel Cleo's second fructosamine appointment because it falls awkwardly around Morgan's visit home and other commitments. I tell the receptionist I will call back to book another appointment, but one day rolls in to the next and I don't.

The Comeback Cat

Does this make me a bad pet owner I wonder, of my decision to not return to the vet right away? But I rationalize. With home glucose testing, I already know what her sugars have been like over the previous weeks. There is part of me that doesn't see the need to also have a fructosamine test which will essentially tell me what I already know.

I check her glucose levels every few days, alternating between her peak and trough times, sometimes skipping more days than I know is right, telling myself it is to give Cleo a break from me poking at her ear, but really I am just discouraged. The numbers barely change and I feel some days like 'what's the point?'

She dips down to 11.5 one day and I am elated. I think we are turning a corner. But the next test is back up at 18.7 and the following tests after that jump around all over the place without any rhyme or reason between 15 and 20.

Cleo continues to slump about the house as February turns to March and our routine stays the same. The first thing I do every morning is retrieve the little glass bottle of insulin from the fridge and roll its cold form between my hands as the sky outside the windows begins to lighten.

Chestnut circles the kitchen in great looping arcs, changing direction whenever I move from the stairs to the fridge to the counter. Cleo, emerging from her box, clomps across the floor and half sits, half lies down outside the bathroom door following my movements with her wide, green eyes.

I fill the delicate syringe from the insulin bottle, making carefully sure to measure exactly 3 units before replacing the orange cap over the thin needle and setting the syringe down on the counter. I push Chestnut aside as I dish out food from the bags in the cupboard and then turn to place the bowls in their usual spots on the floor. Chestnut runs ahead with a sharp meow while Cleo pushes herself up from the floor with some effort and clomps into the bathroom where she eats her meals.

The crunching sounds of breakfast fill the kitchen and the dogs stir restlessly in the entryway. When Cleo is finished, I wait for her to flail back across the kitchen to her box and then I pick up the syringe and remove the orange cap. I kneel beside the box, pet Cleo on the head and gather the skin at the back of her neck to inject the insulin.

"Good kitty," I say and plant a kiss atop her head.

My attention is then turned to the dogs who need to go outside and then return to eat their breakfast in a frenzied mad dash as though it is a race against time, and then I make my own breakfast.

It is the same thing every morning except on the occasions when I am feeling more awake and can muster enough enthusiasm and fortitude to check Cleo's glucose levels, which I do before breakfast and before insulin, recording the number in the back of that outdated planner.

The evening routine is similar with the insulin and the food and the possible glucose test.

At first it all seems like forward momentum. It feels like I am really treating Cleo's diabetes and doing all the right things. Surely it will just be a matter of time before she starts to get better. But three months in to insulin twice a day and almost two months of glucose testing, it feels very much like we are standing still.

When I get a glucose reading of 22 mmol/L on March 3rd, I feel completely defeated.

And then I get mad.

I am tired of cycling through this endless loop, watching Remission Island recede farther and farther across the grey expanse of open ocean. I am doing everything the vet told me to do, but I feel trapped, vanquished, like a mouse in a maze searching out that elusive piece of cheese, forever turning into dead ends. It's like on one hand we are running in place and yet it all seems so passive, like we are supposed to just hold our breath and wait for something to happen, some miraculous change to occur between one dose of insulin in the morning and the second dose at night. I have had enough.

Isn't the definition of insanity doing the same thing over and over again and expecting different results?

I return to the internet, revisit the pages and pages of information through which I waded months ago and got bogged down, got stuck and turned around and overwhelmed. This time I choose my sites more discerningly. This time I have three months of experience with the disease, watching my cat, knowing a bit more about the process. I can skim through sites now and I can disregard a lot of the peripheral opinions and information. I have a specific need so I search with more precision.

I find websites run by vets who specialize in feline diabetes and by others knowledgeable about animal care. The more I read the more I come to understand why diet is the key factor in treating, and even preventing type II diabetes in felines. In big bold letters I read from a number of sources that diabetic cats should never eat kibble. Ever. In fact, kibble is a completely inappropriate diet for healthy cats and is probably what caused Cleo's illness in the first place.

It all has to do with their physiology. It is believed the housecat of today is descended from desert-dwelling animals who lived in Africa and southern Europe where vegetable matter was sparse and small-mammal prey was plentiful. Adapting to that environment, eating what was available, their systems evolved with their diet. Since cat kibble has only been a main food choice since the mid-1900s – a mere blink of an eye in an evolutionary sense – modern cats, just like their ancestors, thrive on a diet high in animal protein, moderate in fat and low in carbohydrates.

Kibble, I read, is essentially junk food, full of stuff cats don't need and can't really use, such as plant-based proteins that their bodies are not designed to deal with. And because kibble is made through an extrusion process, it contains a high amount of digestible carbohydrate, which spikes glucose levels in the blood. A lot of kibble is made from foods with high glycemic indices like corn and potato.

A feline's gastrointestinal tract is not designed to handle dry form, high-fiber foods. It is shorter than that of a dog or human and is ill equipped to handle foods that require a longer digestion process, but honed for pulling nutrients from animal proteins. They are obligatory carnivores. This means, as a species, they can and should subsist on an exclusively meat-based diet.

No wonder I'm not getting anywhere with Cleo's diabetes. I have been feeding her food she physically cannot properly digest and loading her system with carbohydrates. I wished I had pushed this diet thing more with my vet months earlier when Cleo was first diagnosed. If the disease is caught early enough, sometimes just switching the cat's diet to the appropriate food is all that is needed for the animal's body to begin working properly again without the assistance of insulin injections.

Of course, the food that is most recommended is of the homemade variety. I have toyed with this idea for my dogs over the years, never completely committing to it, but for whatever reason I had never considered it for the cats. Maybe this is the time, I think, and begin researching homemade cat food.

I read through various recipes and lengthy descriptions of what to buy, how to prepare the food and how to store it and I quickly feel overwhelmed. Cats seem to have more specific nutritional needs than dogs do and as I read I begin to worry I am not going to get this right. I am going to choose the wrong kind of meat or not put in enough added nutrients. I am not going to be able to keep up with the demand for the food. I picture myself spending every waking moment preparing meals for my cats, so I opt for the more immediate, easier, solution and search online for the recommended prepared canned foods for diabetic cats.

The Comeback Cat

Next I read about tight regulation, which is essentially the way humans treat diabetes, with frequent glucose testing and responding directly to the numbers with the appropriate amount of insulin or food. I had felt this disconnect over the previous months wondering why I couldn't make decisions about insulin and respond to the actual blood glucose numbers I was recording during home testing. It was like I had all the right pieces of a puzzle but they were not fitting together.

I find a chart online listing blood glucose levels in felines and the corresponding amount of insulin that should be administered. I write out all the numbers on a piece of paper and slide it in to my notebook. The idea behind tight regulation is to give the cat's body what it needs in the moment to handle extra glucose in the blood so that eventually the body might relearn how to respond on its own. This is what I had been hoping for, but I had not been giving Cleo the tools she needed to heal.

It is the middle of March when everything changes. That evening I scoop out the contents of a can of cat food in to Cleo's bowl. I chose it specifically for what it doesn't have in it: no starches, potatoes, rice or vegetables. It is plain chicken pate with the requisite added minerals necessary in a cat's diet.

Chestnut gets his own wet food too, scooped out and mashed up in his bowl. He had been on a wet food diet before when he was recovering from a bout of urinary crystals and had seemed much healthier for it, but we eventually fell back in to the habit of feeding him kibble because it was easier and more

The Comeback Cat

affordable. Both cats gobble up their food ravenously, appreciatively.

When Cleo flails and clomps her way across the kitchen to her box after supper, I follow, as I have done after every meal, syringe in hand, and once she is settled in, paws tucked handily beneath her body, I gather the skin at the back of her neck and inject the insulin.

What I should have done was taken a blood glucose reading first. But I have become complacent, robotic even, in my routines. The disappointment of continuously high numbers had me monitoring Cleo less and less frequently, so it wasn't until a day and a half later, four meals of wet food, four shots of insulin, that I checked her blood glucose.

I found Cleo curled into the well she had created on the edge of the beanbag chair. I sat beside her and laid out all the bits and bobs for doing the glucose test. She stretched when I patted her on the head and scratched her neck. I warmed her ear by rubbing it between my fingers and thumb, positioned the cotton ball on the inside edge and then pricked her ear with the lancet and quickly grabbed the glucometer with testing strip in place and watched the tiny globe of blood get sucked up into the channel on the strip.

I put some pressure on Cleo's ear with the cotton ball while I waited for the number to flash on the screen. And then my heart leapt into my throat. The number had dropped 18 points to 2.2 mmol/L.

In a flurry of confused panic, I looked from the orange numbers on the meter, flashing 'Low blood sugar!' to Cleo lying half-snuggled in to the beanbag chair, somewhat stiffly now that I had pricked her ear.

"Crap!" I said, thinking about what the vet had told us about the dangers of hypoglycemia and wasn't there something about the numbers dropping below 3 not being a good thing? And in the event that it did drop that low weren't we supposed to rush her immediately to the vet?

"Are you okay?" I asked Cleo, half expecting an answer. She stared up at me with eyes bright, alert, relaxed, and far from being lethargic.

I ran my hand roughly over her head and down her body and then I poked my finger into the fluffy white fur of her belly and she grumbled. I watched her breathing and she stared at me a bit warily, perhaps wondering if I was going to stick her again with that needle thing.

"You seem fine," I said suspiciously as I stood back and looked at her from a distance, still holding the glucometer. I turned then and dashed downstairs to the kitchen, throwing another glance over my shoulder as I left the room. I went straight to my computer and scrambled through an online search for what is considered a dangerously low blood glucose level in cats.

Hypoglycemia in diabetics is potentially life threatening. I knew this from day one and am mad at myself for being lackadaisical about regularly testing Cleo's glucose levels. She really did seem fine though when I left her on the beanbag chair.

I quickly learn that 2.2 mmol/L, though low, is still within an acceptable range for cats. Reading further, I come across what our vet told us in the beginning of all this, when my brain was already overloaded with information and the full import of what she said did not register. Apparently, standard practice in the veterinary field has been to keep cats slightly hyperglycemic, the rationale being it is better to have slightly elevated levels than plummeting ones that could cause your cat to slip into a coma or disappear into seizures of a hypoglycemic state.

But according to this site if a cat is on the proper wet food diet and on tight regulation of insulin they will not become dangerously hypoglycemic because their body systems are not violently fluctuating around onslaughts of carbohydrates they can't handle.

In fact, states this site, healthy cats exist at a lower blood sugar level than humans, so a reading that is low for humans is normal for cats. Considering most of what we know about feline diabetes is based on what we know about the disease in humans, I can understand why there may have been a lasting confusion about treatments. But I feel like this practice of holding cats in a slightly hyperglycemic state is contributing to the vicious cycle of keeping them in ill health and dependent on insulin injections.

I relax a bit but keep a close eye on Cleo for the rest of the day, disturbing her long naps with a poke or a prod, chatting loudly to her whenever I walk through the living room, and when she appears, clompingly, to the sound of the opening can as I dish out supper, I do not remove the vial of insulin from the fridge. I check Cleo's blood glucose a couple of hours after her meal and record 2.4 in my book.

Chapter 10

Over the next two weeks I stumble down the stairs in the morning, bleary-eyed in the harsh kitchen light with the still wintry darkness pressing in at the windows even as the first day of spring approaches.

I gather the things I need to test her sugars and descend on Cleo in her box which moves frequently now around the kitchen as I search out the best light for seeing the tiny vein in Cleo's ever-reddening ear. She is surprisingly accommodating as I slide the box with her inside along the floor, positioning it just so while Chestnut follows curiously behind probably wondering why I haven't yet spoken. I feel if I don't say anything until I am done with Cleo, it is like I am not really there, as though the day has not yet begun and everyone will wait to spring to life until I acknowledge it has.

The day after the 2.2 mmol/L reading Cleo didn't need any insulin. I checked her blood glucose five times throughout that day, watching it slowly rise towards 8.0 mmol/L by bedtime, still just within the range of not needing an injection according to the chart I had copied from one of the websites I found.

On the second morning when I pricked her ear beneath the harsh kitchen light before breakfast, I got a reading of 9.2 mmol/L, which called for a ½ unit of insulin, much diminished from her regular 3 units. I checked her sugars frequently that day too, writing them down and waiting for a spike that never came. With tight regulation, insulin is given whenever the glucose levels are elevated, not just at pre-described times of the day, which is what we had been doing, so I followed Cleo that day, checking sugars, chart at hand to determine how much insulin to inject, but she never needed any.

With our new schedule, I become diligent about checking her sugars first thing in the morning, finding them slightly elevated so that after breakfast I am waiting with syringe in hand, always a ½ unit, never more than that.

Cleo and I quickly settle in to a rhythm. She waits patiently each morning in her box as I check her sugars, and then midday I find her melted in to the beanbag chair sleeping soundly and sometimes I sneak in and get my sample before she has completely awakened, still groggily stretching after the ordeal as I kiss her head and say, "Good kitty." And then every day before supper I track her down and check again, but her sugars are always good and she never needs an evening injection.

Many times the testing goes smoothly. Sometimes though, it doesn't. There are still the times when Chestnut sticks his nose unhelpfully into Cleo's face and swipes the cotton balls or the glucometer, making the whole thing in to a game. There are times when the blood won't come and I poke and poke and Cleo's brow lowers into a glower and she threatens to be less cooperative. And there are the times when I hit the vein and bright red blood swirls instantly into a growing globe and glugs into the test strip, overflowing it and smearing into her fur and her little ear comes up with a purply-red bruise.

But mostly she and I do fairly well and because the numbers are so encouraging and I see results I want to check frequently, not like before when the numbers barely changed and Cleo seemed to be deteriorating.

It isn't long before the positive numbers I see on the glucose tests start to show themselves physically. Just as I hadn't really noticed Cleo's legs getting worse during the previous months, I am unsure at first that they are beginning to heal. But within a couple of weeks of beginning our new routine, I can't deny Cleo is definitely moving around a lot easier.

Her legs still clomp noisily across the floor, but they aren't as paddle-like as they were. Her front legs seem to be straightening up, looking less like they are made of rubber. She moves from her box in the kitchen to her food dish without having to stop for a rest. She still hesitates on the stairs up to the living room, taking a break every one or two risers, but she seems lighter somehow as though climbing each step is not as much effort as it had been.

And the awkward stairs up to the bedroom, which Cleo had recently decided to ignore, clomping past them as though they did not exist and that a

The Comeback Cat

whole other room was not waiting there to be explored, are suddenly on her radar again. Clearly, she can tell her body is behaving differently even as I wonder if it really is.

I hear Cleo one night on those stairs to the bedroom, her shuffling step on each riser as she contemplates the next one. I prop myself up in bed to watch the space where the stairs emerge into the room, my bedside light casts a yellow glow across the opening in the floor, contrasts with dark shadow where the stairs drop away to the living room.

There is the knock of Cleo's leg bones on the step. I can picture her toing and froing and I will her to appear at the top of the stairs, imagine her little face peeking over the lip of the floor like it used to. More shuffling, more knocking, and then I throw the covers back, pad across the floor and look down to where Cleo's pale face emerges from the black of the room below. I tiptoe carefully down the stairs, skipping the tiny triangle step that causes Cleo so much trouble and where she rests her front paws, and I scoop her up and carry her to the bedroom, place her on the bed amongst the blankets and then crawl back in beside her.

Cleo settles in for the night, a quiet purr filling the silence of the room as I continue to read and I imagine she is saying thank you.

I watch her body get stronger by leaps and bounds over the next while. Her front legs heal quickly, regaining their straight and strong bearing, while her back legs repair minimally each day. One day she is no longer flailing and clonking across the floor but moving more confidently, a waddle to her back end as she encourages her back legs to keep up, her hocks coming off the floor incrementally.

I know for a fact she is feeling better when doing the blood testing becomes more difficult. No longer so eagerly cooperative, there are some days when Cleo fights me off. She never bites or resorts to nasty behaviour, but she is ready for me, hunkering down when she sees me coming with all the paraphernalia, twisting her head this way and that as I try to place the cotton ball in her ear, swatting at my hand as I approach with the lancing device, folding her ears back, pulling away last minute, and occasionally grumbling a protest deep down in her throat.

It is as though she thinks this thing that was once necessary, that provided some kind of hope for healing, is no longer needed. 'This is ridiculous,' she probably thinks. 'I feel fine now, except for this pain in my ear.'

Just two days shy of three weeks after Cleo started eating wet food, she gets her last shot of insulin, a ½ unit after breakfast. With her body kick-started back to action, her sugars level out around 4.0 mmol/L, bouncing back and forth across that line, sometimes higher, but never more than 6.3 mmol/L.

We have officially made it to remission. This does not mean Cleo is cured though. Once a cat is diabetic it is always diabetic. Her body may have recalibrated itself to handle glucose in the blood stream and even heal the nerve damage caused as a side effect of the illness, but it does not mean everything won't fall apart again if we go back to doing what we were doing before. In other words,

The Comeback Cat

Cleo can never eat kibble again or she will immediately revert back to her unhealthy state.

Remission is a victory none-the-less and Cleo celebrates by finally tackling the stairs to the bedroom on her own. She shuffles and clomps her way up the stairs each night to join me. At first I have to lift her on to the mattress, but gradually she is able to do it herself, appearing on the bed with the beginnings of a spring in her step as she storms across the blankets with her intense green eyes trained on my face, her mouth opening to squeak out a greeting in her little half voice that also seems to be getting stronger.

Each night she curls up beside my pillow in the space where Morgan's pillow would be if he were home, and settles in for the night. It is as though she is letting me know she is grateful. That's what it feels like. She is thanking me for taking care of her, helping her heal and for finally getting to know her.

I discover her mid-April, galloping around the kitchen with her toy mouse. Its ears, two little circles of green felt folded in half and glued together, sit on the kitchen table beside the teapot after Molly ripped them off the day before. Cleo doesn't mind though. She swipes at the gold and burgundy striped body and sends it sliding across the floor. Then she leaps after it, her back legs working hard as they clonk against the hardwood every other step, wheeling behind her still as though she is wearing oversized shoes on her feet.

Another day I walk into the kitchen to find Cleo poised on the very periphery of the kitchen table. Her front paws grip the edge with her back feet placed firmly on either side of them, a neat row of dainty white paws. She pitches forward a bit so all her weight is on her front paws and she bobs her head out over the empty space between herself and the kitchen counter, stretching her neck as if gauging the distance. Her nose twitches, the muscles of her back legs contract beneath her patchy fur, bum wiggling ever so slightly, tail curled casually behind her inches above the table as a counter balance.

Directly beneath her, at the bottom of the chasm across which she is attempting to leap, lies Murdoch. His black shaggy shape is sprawled on the floor, filling the entire space. He is dozing in the warmth of the kitchen, but I know him and to me he is a dragon guarding a castle. He seems unaware of Cleo standing directly above him, but if she falls, doesn't quite make the jump and lands on the dragon, all hell will break loose. There will be snarling and snapping and fur flying. It is as though Cleo has specifically chosen this moment, with the dog there, to test her abilities, challenge herself, make her day more exciting.

She is not allowed on the table or the counter, but I don't interrupt her. I am curious if she can make the jump. I want to see this. My heart is light. I am silently cheering for her.

It is quite a jump and up until recently I would have laughed at her bravado, her insistence that she could do this if she really wanted to, imagining her plummeting like a stone mid-jump, dragged down by her weight, paws scrabbling at the air still feet from her destination. But since her recovery over the past few months, her recovery and then some, reverting back really to when she was two and was slim and sleek and full of energy. I think if she really tried, if she really mustered up the right amount of bounce in her step, she could make it.

She teeters forward again and then back. There is the almost imperceptible contraction of every muscle in her body and then she is leaping, sailing through the air in a perfect arc, body elongated, white belly stretched long, high above the sleeping dragon who takes no notice of this airborne snack. She lands squarely on the counter with barely a sound and casually strolls along the edge, nonchalance streaming off of her.

"You must feel like a superstar," I tell her, scooping her from the counter and plopping her in my lap as I sit at the kitchen table. On the floor at my feet Murdoch stretches with a contented groan. Cleo bumps me roughly on the chin with the top of her head and I take her face in my hands and kiss her forehead, scratch her ears. "But you're not allowed on the counter."

Cleo trills in her throat, bumps her body against my chest as though bestowing me with a hug and now she jumps lightly to the floor and tiptoes effortlessly across the kitchen with purpose as though looking for the next challenge to conquer, ready to take on the world.

Her energy levels grow exponentially each day, and as spring emerges, melts out of the receding snow, I feel a sense of loss for the life these cats have not had. I imagine what it would have been like if Cleo had succumbed to her diabetes, stumbling awkwardly, embarrassingly towards death and never having really lived. Imagine spending your days inside the same building, staring at the same walls, while life happened right outside the windows.

The cats have spent nine years indoors glimpsing the exterior world through the legs of the dogs as they march in and out, breathing the outside air while pushed up against the screen door, making the occasional dash across the threshold into the woods beyond to be hunted down and returned unceremoniously to the "inside".

We haven't let them out on purpose in years, after the songbird body count started to rise each time the cats slunk about beneath the trees. And then there was the mildly questionable diagnosis of feline immunodeficiency virus that I imagined left them open to all sorts of fatal ailments, not to mention the very real possibility that they would be eaten by something, and not just the wolves we heard howling on the mountain on cool, dark nights or the foxes we had occasionally seen skipping past our windows, there are eagles out there too and ravens, and there are horned owls nesting somewhere in our woods whose low, soft voices pulse through the trees at the same time every morning and every evening.

We thought it was best for everyone's health and safety for the cats to stay indoors.

But now, after Cleo's brush with death and what, to me, feels like an almost miraculous resurgence of energy, I begin to rethink some things. Suddenly it seems terribly unfair that these creatures with their partial wild streak should never be allowed to wander free amongst the trees, to be allowed to do what they naturally do.

The Comeback Cat

So I decide one sunny morning in late May to let them go outside.

They explode out the door like it is the great escape, like they are getting away with something, and scatter once they are off the deck, heading down the rocky path towards the driveway and off into the sparsely growing underbrush of spring. I stand on the deck and watch them go while the dogs jostle for position at the door behind me.

I spend most of my day keeping tabs on the cats. I leave them alone for five minutes here, ten there and then I am wandering down the path again calling their names. I see them from a distance sitting on a log in the sun. Later I find one of them skulking through the underbrush beside the house, the other sprawled in the dirt of the driveway.

I follow them through the trees, talking to them, telling them to not go too far and to not kill any birds. Cleo is not quite walking right yet and when I find the cats near the road, I watch as they wander together along the edge where the grass grows in from the ditches, Chestnut with his fluid lion-like stride and Cleo waddling out front. And then Cleo takes off at a run. It is awkward and lumbering and full of effort and when she stops, she lies down at the top of our neighbours' driveway to rest. But I see her do it again later and it is as though she is trying out her legs again after they haven't worked for so long.

I feel good about them being outdoors, though I do not settle in to the idea easily and spend the following weeks jumping up every so often to peer out of windows and try to catch glimpses of them flashing through the trees, taking random walks around the house, strolling into the bush, down the driveway, listening for rustling leaves or the occasional distant meow. And every day when they return to the house, I am relieved that the last time I saw them, skulking down the path midday, would not be the last time I saw them.

By the time Morgan returns in June from his time away, Cleo is a completely different cat. She is more social, visiting the neighbours at their house semi-regularly and running to meet people who appear in our driveway, with her loud and purposeful meow fully restored. She likes to be seen now where as before she did not, preferring to take a more disgruntled role in our home.

Cleo seems to be taking this second chance at life quite seriously. Not only has she regained the full use of her body but also her personality is decidedly more sunny than it once was. She has become more personable and actually seems to enjoy the company of others, seeking out a lap instead of disappearing in to the far corners of the house to reappear at meal times, lively chatting to me about her day instead of sitting quietly in the kitchen and staring almost disapprovingly, most definitely judgingly, at the life unfolding there.

One day while I am walking my dogs, Cleo appears on the trail in our woods as if she has always been there, as if this trail is well known to her and in fact belongs to her and she is just letting us use it out of the kindness of her tiny feline heart.

She looks like she belongs there too, after I get over the initial urge to scoop her up and run her back to the house. We hear her meow before we see her, the dogs and I. We meander our way between the trees leaving our house behind in search of adventure on our daily walk. It is a grey day and the light falls heavy and flat to the forest floor and the harsh, ringing meow coming from the underbrush seems to cast the flatness of the light in to sharp relief.

It is slightly jarring to hear Cleo's crisp voice breaking the serenity of the woods and when she appears, she seems bigger than I would have imagined her to be amongst the trees, but she also seems to be well camouflaged in her mottled coat of leafy beige and grey the colour of storm clouds.

"Reowr," she says again as she sets her green eyes on the three of us and marches down the trail to meet us, white legs flashing.

"Hello Cleo," I say, bending down to pet her head as she leaps up to meet my hand with a trill and a couple of short meows. "What are you doing way up here?"

And she looks at me with a look that is both knowing and filled with secrets.

"You should go back to the house," I say, always thinking about what might be lurking behind trees that would find a house cat just the perfect thing to abate pangs of hunger. But she trots happily beside us for a few moments, any thought of returning home or leaving the woods clearly not even a glimmer in her mind.

When we reach the fork in the trail, the dogs and I turn left on a path that will follow the edge of our square of woods where it butts up to the clamour of white poplar saplings that jostle for space in the new growth forest beside our property and eventually turn towards the mountain.

Cleo loiters at the fork, contemplating her options. I glance back over my shoulder, curious if she will follow. But instead she trots off in to the woods where there is no clear trail, moving with the relaxed purpose of someone with a plan pretending to not have a plan, just like a cat.

Epilogue

It is just one month shy of a year after Cleo was diagnosed with type II diabetes, seven months since she received her last shot of insulin and eight since she and Chestnut started their new wet food only diet. The cats are 10 years old and have never been healthier.

Chestnut is slimming down and Cleo is filling out again. She dropped her weight so fast when she got sick, her skin hung from her body like a carpet draped over a laundry line. Her spine protruded so my fingers ridged along it whenever I ran my hand down her back. As she rebuilds fat stores and muscle mass, her body becomes soft again around the edges and she begins to look like a much younger cat.

I continue to do random glucose tests to make sure her sugars are not climbing, but most days I can tell just by looking at her that she is still on track. I am obsessed with how she's walking – fine – how often she gets tired – typical amount for a cat – if she's drinking too much water – not at all.

The Comeback Cat

Cleo tiptoes quietly through the kitchen now and leaps effortlessly on to the couch. She climbs to the top of the beanbag chair as though scaling a mountain, no longer needing the low-slung shelf she carved for herself. She races with reckless abandon up the stairs to the top of the house and then down again and she joins Chestnut in the hungry march before meal times, flitting from one side of the kitchen to the other, a robust meow voicing her excitement as she runs ahead to the spot on the floor where her food dish is always placed and then prances in circles until I put it in front of her.

She spends time each day telling me important things with her matter-of-fact meow, circling my legs as I walk through a room, staring up at me with intense green eyes full of thoughts to be relayed if I would just stop a moment and listen, which I do. I bend down, hand outstretched to pet her and she leaps up to meet it, standing on her back tiptoes, her head colliding roughly with my palm.

She doesn't panic like she used to when I scoop her up into my arms, give her a hug, carry her to another room. She finds spare moments to crawl into my lap and sit for a spell, sometimes leaning against my chest, bumping my chin with the top of her head.

And there are some mornings when Cleo creeps quietly, but not too quietly, into the bedroom to walk the periphery in the grey light of dawn, her mottled fur blending with the shadowed room, her feet padding softly on wood. She springs lightly on to the bed and settles down on my chest, her pale face inches from my own, and I pretend to sleep as she purrs her gentle, whisper of a purr, and the sky begins to lighten outside the windows.

Resources

The following is a short list of the websites I found most helpful when learning about feline diabetes and treating Cleo:

www.yourdiabeticcat.com
Information about importance of diet and how to manage feline diabetes through tight regulation of insulin.

www.felinediabetes.com/diabetes-info.htm
A comprehensive explanation, in plain language, of what is happening in the body of a diabetic cat.

www.catinfo.org
Abundance of information about feline nutrition and how poor diets affect health.

www.preventivevet.com/cats/your-cat-and-diabetes-everything-you-need-to-know
Basic overview of feline diabetes.

www.peteducation.com/article.cfm?c=1+2130&aid=199
Basic overview of feline diabetes.

pathwithpaws.com/blog/2012/06/04/prevention-of-crystals-in-cats-and-a-little-about-flutd-some-holistic-thoughts-about-diet-and-treatment/
Information about diet and urinary crystals in cats.

Thanks!

This may be a small book and it may not have taken half a lifetime to write, but still I feel compelled to thank a few people who have encouraged its writing, who read early drafts, who jumped in with enthusiasm when mine had waned.

Thank you Gerry and Ian, Tanis and Susan, and always mom and dad for your encouragements with not only this book but for all the writing I have ever done and will ever do.

And thank you Morgan, for if you had never brought home that box of kittens, this story would not exist.

About the author

Heather Peden is a freelance writer and nature photographer. She lives with her husband, their dogs, and cats in the woods outside Thunder Bay, Ontario. This is her first book.

More stories about life with her animals can be found on her blog Three Dogs and a Couch (threedogsandacouch.blogspot.ca).

www.ingramcontent.com/pod-product-compliance
Lightning Source LLC
Chambersburg PA
CBHW020908090426
42736CB00008B/534